New Techniques That Catch More Bluegill

Steve L. Wunderle

1983
WUNDERLE OUTDOOR BOOKS
86 Eight Mile Prairie Road
Carterville, IL 62918

It is with great respect, appreciation, and admiration that I dedicate this book to Paul Johnson of Spirit Lake, Iowa. A unique individual who not only has pioneered new frontiers in Sportfishing to make you a better angler, but introduced me into a new world of underwater diving and outdoor writing. An unpretentious gentleman that asks nothing from you, not even your respect of him, but you will give it without hesitation.

© 1983 by STEVE L. WUNDERLE

SIXTH EDITION

Library of Congress Card Number: 83-90963

Published by Steve Wunderle, Wunderle Outdoor Books, Carterville, Illinois 62918

Acknowledgements

I wish to thank many dedicated bluegill anglers, fisheries biologists, outdoor writers, and friends who made this publication possible. This book leans heavily upon their expert knowledge and advice. To them I express my sincere thanks.

A very special appreciation goes to several people and companies that supported my efforts. Mr. Jack Holderfield, who is a wizard in the darkroom, did an outstanding job of printing the photos used in this book. My very good friend, Joe Sawicki of Carbondale, Illinois, who provided technical support and computer advice. Mr. Larry Jacober of Carbondale passed on some very helpful techniques which made writing this book on the Apple computer easier. Dr. Roy Heidinger of the Fisheries Department at Southern Illinois University for supplying research information and advice for this book. Outstanding outdoor writer and good friend, Bill Sargent of Melbourne, Florida, who shared information and aided me in taking some critical photos. Tony Dean of the great In-Fisherman Radio series for supplying key information on northern bluegill fishing. Lefty Kreh for providing me with some key bluegill fly fishing tips. Mr. Jerry DeSoto, English instructor at John A. Logan College, critically read an important chapter of this book. Scuba diver, Jay Zapp of Carbondale, Illinois, who assisted me on numerous underwater dives. Steve Bradley, a young artist from Carterville, Illinois, furnished a deep water bluegill drawing. The Illinois Department of Conservation Fisheries Division for providing drawings.

I am grateful to the following for providing different types of support so that interviews for the book could take place. Berkley and Company provided me laboratory time at their Spirit Lake plant to conduct line and knot research. Also Steve Vogts of Berkley not only provided information, but some key photos of fishing for summer bluegill. Sam Waltz, public relations representative for the Stren Division of the Dupont Company, made arrangements for the Bill Dance interview material used in this book. Tommy Akin, Keeper Bait Company, made arrangements for my Reelfoot Lake, Tennessee material and several bottles of Fish Formula II for my testing and observations. Ray Goodman of Timberline and Tackle, Marion, Illinois for information on the care of live bait. Bob Knopf of Berkley and Company for providing drawings.

The following companies provided technical support and I am very appreciative: Susan Bibler of Juhl Associates for Garcia and Red Ball, Bing McClellan of Zebco, Gordon Andrews of Lew Childre and Company, Bing McClellan of Burke Fishing Lures, Joe Cook of Comet Tackle, Sheldons' Inc. makers of Mepps Spinners, Thayne Smith at Lowrance Electronics, Al Buck of Buck Knives, David Maiser of Lindy-Little Joe, Christine Case-Anderson of Chicago Cutlery, Sandy Kaye (President of Porta-Bote International), Magic Products (makers of Magic Worm Bedding), Gatorbait Company, Keeper Bait Company, John Campbell of Tru-Turn Hooks, Randy Harris of Brinkmann Company, Al Hamilton of Arrowhead Lodge, and Bill Shinkle of Boardman Resort.

Introduction

Fishing resides in a small crevice of your mind. It is a private place that we escape for a few fleeting minutes each day to reminisce, plot and skeme our past and present fishing trips. It is a pleasant mental state where we can escape the pressures of life. Unless you love and have lived in the great outdoors, then this private and personal sanctuary doesn't exist. You have indeed missed knowing and having a special kind of inner peace that only comes from fishing.

Bluegill fishing is very special to me. This scrapper was the first fish I started chasing in the backwaters of the Illinois river. It was quite a thrill then as it is now to catch these fish. It is even more enjoyable to share this excitement with a young angler who will someday learn to use the great outdoors as a mental escape as I do.

Bluegill angling is meant to be enjoyed with light tackle. A rod and reel should not be thought of as a winch to "haul" a bluegill into the boat. Instead light tackle should be used to enjoy the subtle powers of this most enjoyable fish.

So sit back and take an exciting trip into the underwater world of the bluegill. Why is it exciting you ask? Because this book is going to make you a better bluegill angler forever!

New Techniques
That Catch More Bluegill

by STEVE L. WUNDERLE

CHAPTER 1

Biology of The Bluegill

The bluegill **(Lepomis macrochirus)** is regarded as one of the most esteemed and sought-after panfish in the continental waters of the United States. In fact, many anglers and state conservation departments will tell you that more individuals fish for bluegill than for any other freshwater fish. There are a number of good reasons for this assumption, the most important being its wide distribution and its abundance in all waters.

Due to the bluegill's wide range and abundance, this fish offers sportfishing to anglers of all ages and varying levels of skill. Most of us at a very tender age were treated to this addictive sport when our bobber slipped silently under the water due to a voracious bluegill tugging on a worm baited hook.

Many anglers reading this book will want to skip over this chapter on the biology of the bluegill and get right to the heart of catching this exciting fish. I personally believe that this would be a serious error on your part because to understand how to catch any given fish species, you must know a little about them and their habits. This chapter lays very important background information to make you a better bluegill angler forever!

The bluegill, like so many fishes, assumes a variety of popular names depending upon the local jargon. The name bluegill is the most widely accepted name. However, it is also known as bream, blue bream, blue fish, blackear bream, blue, bluemouth sunfish, coppernosed sunfish, sunfish, sun perch, and the males have even been called strawberry bass because of their rust colored breasts.

Bluegills are members of the sunfish family (Centrachidae) which include some of the most popular freshwater sportfish in the United States. Members of this family include the white crappie, black crappie, warmouth, green sunfish, rock bass, long-eared sunfish, redeared sunfish, smallmouth bass, and one of the dominant predators of the bluegill, the black bass.

The bluegill originally ranged from southern Ontario, south through the Great Lakes and Mississippi drainages to the Gulf of Mexico, to northeastern Mexico and over to Florida, and finally up the coast to the Carolinas. Today they are found in virtually every state because of their widespread introductions. Even Europe and South Africa share the excitement of this species. Once introduced, this fish is very adaptable to the habitat and food supply that it encounters. This fish is capable of living in such habitats as lakes, rivers, streams, back-waters off the main river channels, and farm ponds.

Description

Bluegill can and do vary greatly in coloration depending upon their environment. In fact, they vary so much in color patterns that they are readily confused with other species of the sunfish family.

This fish is deep and much compressed laterally. The depth of an adult bluegill is slightly less than half of the body length. The body is seldom more than an inch thick even on the most robust of specimens.

This fish varies a great deal in coloration. The basic color ranges from yellow to dark blue. Generally, they have a dark olive-green back with purple or an iridescent blue vertical or irregular shaped bars which total six to eight in number on each side of the fish. The breast of the female is white or an anemic yellow, whereas the male's breast is yellow or a reddish-orange. The chin and lower part of the gill cover of both sexes is blue.

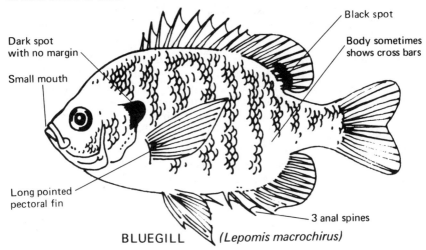

Black spot

Body sometimes shows cross bars

Dark spot with no margin

Small mouth

Long pointed pectoral fin

3 anal spines

BLUEGILL   *(Lepomis macrochirus)*

PRINTED BY PERMISSION FROM THE ILLINOIS DEPARTMENT OF CONSERVATION, FISHERIES DIVISION.

The bluegill has a short black ear flap with no red spot like one finds on its cousin the redear. The pectoral fin is rather long pointed and reaches well past the front of the eye when bent forward across the eye. The anal fin has three spines and 10-12 soft rays and the tail is forked with rounded tips. The dorsal fin has 10 spines and 10-12 soft rays with a black spot found at the posterior end of the dorsal fin.

The mouth of the bluegill is small and this makes it very difficult for anglers to extract hooks when swallowed by over eager fish. Fishermen should always use a hook which will match the size of the bluegill. If the hook is too large, small bluegill will strip the live bait off and the bobber may not even go under the surface of the water.

Growth

Newly hatched bluegill average only two to three millimeters in length. However, during the next three years of their life they begin a very rapid growth period and can attain a length of six inches. In some waters these fish will grow to over six and one half inches in four years. The average adult can measure from five to nine inches and tip the scales at a half-pound when it reaches seven years of age. Generally speaking, larger bluegill are found in new ponds and reservoirs where growth is most rapid and slowest in turbid or overpopulated ponds. Stunting commonly occurs in the latter situation.

However, slow and rapid growth of this fish has been reported from both the southern and northern states. The size of the bluegill population and other habitat conditions, including the food supply, seem to play a more important role in growth than does the growing season or latitude. Research indicates that more rapid growth occurs in the southern states than the north. The life span of this fish species seems to be greater in the northern part of its range.

Males can grow generally more rapidly than females in some populations, but the differences were usually small. According to the research, very little sexual differences in growth has been detected in most areas of the country.

Growth of young fish depends upon the amount of feeding that occurs during the year. Very little feeding and no growth occurs in the bluegill below 50-55 degree fahrenheit. Most of the growth occurs above 68 degrees. Very little growth was found at temperatures over 80 degree even though the fish were still feeding.

A bluegill that lives to be over seven years of age is an old timer, even though there are records of bluegill as old as 13 years. The largest bluegill ever caught on hook and line was 4 pounds, 12 ounces and measured 15 inches. This trophy, caught by T. S. Hudson on April 9, 1950, was taken from Ketona Lake, Alabama.

GROWTH RATE OF BLUEGILL

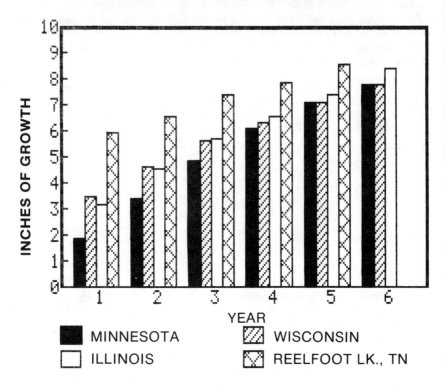

What lakes hold trophy bluegill? That question is not easily answered. A productive lake is a complex. interlocked chain of plant and animal life. A proper amount of nutrients must be present to stimulate the entire food chain, but not too much to cause excessive algae and water weed growth

A successful pond or lake has to have a good supply of microscopic animals, insect larvae, small crustaceans, and small minnows. Bluegills must have a source of food to grow in length, put on weight, and develop sexually. Thus lake fertility plays a very important role in producing big bluegill. Strip mine lakes, with their clear and rather sterile water, will hold bluegill but not many jumbo bream. Lakes such as Horseshoe Lake in Illinois and Reelfoot Lake in Tennessee produce thousands of pounds of big bream. These lakes are so rich in small animal life that you can scoop up many organisms out of the weedlines.

The ratio of deep water to shallow water is important in determining the total weight of fish produced. Shallow water will always produce more plant and animal life than deep water areas because of the greater penetration of the sunlight.

Most big bluegill lakes are characterized by a very good population of small bass. A few lunker bass may be present, but the lake is loaded with packs of small bass always looking for a meal of small bluegill. Thus the bluegill are kept in check and many of them can and do grow to trophy quality.

Where do I spend my time bluegill fishing? I select ponds or lakes that are fertile and have a large population of small bass. The lake should also have a good spawning area of sand or gravel.

Food Habits

While young bluegill eat small water fleas and algae, the adult feeds primarily on aquatic insects such as midge fly larvae. The adults of the midge larvae resemble large mosquitos and often appear in clouds over the lake in the summer. Those anglers who have motored in off the lake at dusk know what midge fly adults are since they smack against your face and stick in your teeth. Small crayfish and even small fish also make up part of their diet.

A fallen tree is an ideal location for young bluegill to feed upon water fleas and aquatic insect larvae. The adult bluegill feed primarily on the aquatic insects such as midge fly larvae.

Bluegill will often eat aquatic vegetation as a roughage. I have found numerous bluegill with vegetation in their stomachs. Research has shown that bluegill get some energy from algae and even grow better when this was part of their diet. The increase of plant material in their diet during the summer months has caused some researchers to speculate that this may be one of the main reasons for the reduced catchability of bluegills by anglers.

Spawning Behavior

Spawning generally means that the angler's "luck" has just started to improve. According to my good friend and excellent outdoor writer, Bill Sargent of Palm Bay, Florida, this good "luck" will start as early as mid-March at Lake Okeechobee and last well into early fall. In the northern United States spawning doesn't start until early June and generally continues until early August. Spawning times for other areas of the United States will fall in between these dates.

Cued by a water temperature of 67 degrees, male or bull bluegills usually select a sand or gravel bottom to hollow out a nest bowl. Other types of bottoms are used in waters that lack such sandy or gravely bottoms. Nests are usually in areas exposed to the sun but often in the shade of trees. It is not uncommon for the same nesting area to be used for several seasons. When this occurs, the male does not have to build a new nest the next year but instead he fans out the old site and picks up gravel with his mouth and moves this debris to the outer rim of the bedding site.

BLUEGILL SPAWNING SEASON IN THE UNITED STATES

STATE	SPAWNING SEASON
Florida	February to October
Texas	March to September
Alabama	April to October
Oklahoma	Middle of April to Middle of July
Illinois	May to September
Ohio	Early May to Middle of August
Missouri	Late May to September
Wisconsin	Late May to Early August
Michigan (Upper Peninsula)	Early June to Early September

The nesting site is two to six inches in depth and approximately one foot in diameter. I have measured some spawning nests that were 18-25 inches in width. Usually many nests are located close together in a limited area. It is not uncommon for several females to use the same nest. A female may also deposit her eggs in more than one nest.

The nest bowl is fanned by violent swishes of the body and caudal fin. Even though the other nest may be almost touching each other, the males vigorously defend the nesting territory. They are in a constant state of chasing other males and attempting to attract females to the nesting site. In extremely clear water, it is easy to drive the males and females from these nesting areas, however they will return in a few minutes if you back your boat off a short distance from the nesting site.

As a young boy, my brother Terry and I would crawl to a bed of blue-gill and lay the bait in the middle of the nesting site. Feeding out line as we crawled backwards, we would wait for several minutes until the aggressive males would make their way back to protect their nest. Upon finding an earthworm in the middle of their bed, they would quickly pick up the intruder only to find a hook biting into the corner of their mouth. Many bluegills would decorate our bicycle as we started our long trek home out of the bottoms.

Male bluegill go through an elaborate courtship and defense of the nesting territory. The defending male orients its head toward the other fish with its dorsal, anal, and pelvic fins erect. He will generally make a quick thrust towards the intruder and retreat into his nest. If the intruder gets to close, the defending male will chase it and sometimes the chase terminates in a nip. The defending fish then returns to its nest site.

Once at the nest site, the male will repeatedly swim in circles around the rim of his nest with his fins in a displaying posture. The male in a horizontal position begins to sweep the nest site with his caudal fins in

A spawning bed area with the males actively guarding their nest bowl. The females had not moved into the bedding area even though the water temperature was 71 degrees.

a side-to-side manner, curving his body upward until the body is almost vertical (head up). This sweeping action of the caudal fin forms a depression.

When spawning nears, the male continues to hover over the nest bowl and circle the rim of the site. Attracted by the swimming action of the males, females swollen with eggs swim from deep water. A female will be chased and encircled by the male. The female generally does not show the same enthusiasm which is exhibited by the male. She remains rather indifferent to the entire event. The male encircles her and gently guides her to the nest. Once in the nest the female will chose to leave or remain. If she swims away, the male will chase her and attempt to attract her back. However, once the female stays on the bed, the act of courtship has been completed.

Once settled in the nest, the male swims close beside her and they face in the same direction and circle the nest together. While circling the nest, the male remains upright, but the female tilts the top of her body away from the male. Leaning to one side, she rubs the ventral surface near her genital pore in a very fast "vibrating" movement against the side of the male near his anal fin. She tilts her body in this spawning posture every 60-100 seconds. As contact is made, sperm mixes with about 12,000-40,000 eggs. The entire spawning session may take from 15-90 minutes.

The male maintains a constant vigil and keeps the eggs aerated and clean by a gentle fanning with his fins. Hatching of the eggs takes only two to five days under normal weather conditions. The male will protect the school of fry for several more days.

CHAPTER 2

How to Catch Bluegill During the Spawning Season

Expert bluegill anglers will tell you that the secret of catching big bulls, and lots of them, is knowing when and where to seek these scrappy fighters. Some anglers will even tell you that they can smell out a good spawning area because of all the bluegill present in a given area. For those of us who lack such bird dog noses, we have to learn where and when they are vulnerable to our maximum efforts.

We can catch jumbo bluegill during the tough summer season and a complete chapter has been devoted to this effort, however, only once a year are these fish concentrated to such an extent that we can and do fill our freezers with some prime eating. When the bluegill invade the shallows during the spring, the spawning season is not far behind. For a few weeks, these fish are extremely catchable with different types of tackle.

Many bass anglers feel that the lowly bluegill does not offer a challenge to them. Anyone who doesn't love fishing for bedding bluegill and the thrill of a bobber slipping below the surface, just doesn't enjoy the great outdoors to its maximum. Bluegill fishing is not just kids play, but it should be enjoyed by everyone.

Most of us know that spawning is triggered by an increasing water temperature and day length. However, there are a number of excellent anglers who claim that a full moon is even more important to their fishing success.

As the water temperature starts climbing into the mid-sixties, male bluegill start working their way into the shallows to set up housekeeping. There is no great urgency to start fanning a bed until the water temperature approaches 67 or 68 degrees. Meanwhile, they are feeding heavily on aquatic insects so their gonads can increase in size and mature. While all of this pre-spawn activity is going on, the length of each passing day is having a major influence on the maturation of the eggs of the female and the sperm of the male.

A Full Moon May Trigger Spawning

"A full moon may be what really triggers bluegill spawning," according to outdoor writer Bill Sargent of Palm Bay, Florida. Sargent recently interviewed one of best bluegill and redear anglers in the state of Florida. Bill said that Dewey Bradley, a sixty-eight year-old panfish angler from Coffee County, Alabama, catches more big redears and bluegills in a four month period than most anglers catch in a lifetime.

This Pensacola resident fishes deep within the reed beds with his favorite fish-getter, a long cane pole. According to Sargent, this angler fishes every day of the year, rain or shine, from the first of February to the end of May on Lake Okeechobee.

"The best fishing is always in the week after the full moon because that's when the fish are really hungry," quotes Sargent in his conversation with Bradley.

"During the week before full moon the males are moving in and out of shallow, sandy bottom areas, scouting and looking, until they find the place they want the females to bed. When they find the right spot, they go in and fan out the beds," he explained.

Like clock work Bradley found that "On the day of the full moon, the females come into the beds and they'll stay there that night and until noon the next day. Then they're gone, until the next full moon."

Bradley went on to explain to Sargent that "The males stay with the nest, to guard it, and they'll be there for a week to ten days. That's when they'll bite. They haven't taken time to eat since they started looking for the beds and they're hungry. That first week after full moon is when you'll catch a batch."

What is even more interesting, Bradley claims that each female lays eggs three times, on each of the full moons for three consecutive months. In that area of Florida the heaviest bedding is usually in March, April and May, with May the best month out of the three.

Bradley is one of those individuals that smell bluegill beds. "A lot of people tell me I can't do it, but I can definitely smell bream when they're bedding. I do it all the time. They smell just like a gob of fish. I ease along in my boat and when I smell'em I drop anchor and start fishin' a circle to find the nest. You don't have to believe me, but it works."

Fisheries researchers in central Florida have found that the synchronous spawning period of redears indicate that bedding activity is triggered by some stimulus to which all the population would be equally subjected. They found that many shellcracker anglers strongly contend that bedding is affected by moon phase, and the shellcrackers spawn on the new and/or full moon. Dates of spawning on Lake Griffin in 1969 showed the following:

Spawned March 14 to 17 - New moon March 18
Spawned April 1 to 5 - Full moon April 2
Spawned April 18 to 22 - New moon April 16
Spawned May 1 to 7 - Full moon May 2
Spawned June 25 to 31 - Full moon June 29

According to fisheries biologist Robert L. Wilbur, "While the above data indicate that moon phases may affect shellcracker spawning, the correlation may be coincidental, and further study is needed."

Underwater diver, Jay Zapp of Carbondale, Illinois, has told me for several years that he finds active spawning beds of bluegill during the periods of a full moon. This scuba diver prowls many of the clear stripmine lakes in southern Illinois where bass and bluegill dominate the fish populations.

May 23, 1982 I joined Zapp underwater in a stripmine cut that had numerous bluegill present. The water was a warm 76 degrees and most area lakes had bluegill spawning since the 7th of May, which was the first day of the full moon. However, as we approached an underwater island at the 15 foot level, we saw 15-20 beds which were swept clean and ready for spawning but no activity was found. Later we checked the calendar to find out that it was one day after a new moon. Zapp quickly pointed out that these beds would be buzzing with activity on the 6th of June which would be the next full moon.

Bubbles Will Lead You to Spawning Bluegill

No one travels more throughout the United States fishing for different fish species than Bill Dance. Bill loves to fish for bluegill, in fact he enjoys angling for anything that will jerk his fishing rod.

Bill told me that when the water temperature reaches the upper sixties or low seventies several days before a full moon, this is when you can expect bedding to take place. The female will come into the bedding area and spawn out, leave the area, but the male remains to guard the nesting area.

How does Bill locate some of his better bedding areas? He watches for frothy bubbles on the surface of the water. As these bubbles arise to the surface of the water, they remain for long periods of time.

Some guides feel that the bubbling is done through the mouth of the male bluegill during nest bed preparation and spawning. However, in a conversation with Dr. Roy Heidinger, Fisheries Researcher at Southern Illinois University, he pointed out that the air bladder of the bluegill is not connected with its mouth. Therefore, Dr. Heidinger feels that possibly the bubbling is a result of the trapped gases being released to

Frothy bubbles rise to the surface of a very active spawning bed.

the surface by the nest building action of the male. The frothiness of the bubbles may come about by these gas bubbles rising through the mucous secretions of the male.

I first saw this bubbling on Reelfoot Lake. I was sharing a boat with guide Benny Smith when he pointed this action out to me. We were able to catch bluegill everywhere it occurred that day.

Several days later in southern Illinois, I went to my favorite bluegill lake to see if this bubbling phenomenon occurred. Sure enough there it was and the bluegill were very much into nest building. In fact, the bubbles were so numerous that a frothy scum was building up on the shoreline.

A fluke you say? Two days later I traveled to my clear stripmine lake to observe and photograph spawning bluegill. Bubbles were rising more from the tail sweeping action of the bluegill rather than from the mouth. The next day the spawning pocket was covered with so much mucous scum that you could not see the beds.

This bubbling phenomenon is for real and should be an important part of your fish plan. Dance uses these frothy bubbles to his advantage when fishing a spawn bed.

Frothy bubbles and surface scum indicate a very active bed of spawning bluegill. The cover for this book was taken under this dock during
the summer.

"The key to fishing a bed and catching a high percentage of bluegill
off that bed is to fish the bed from the outside in," disclosed Dance.
The bubbles give him clues as to the size of the bed. "When you drop a
cricket in the middle of a bed, that fighting male is going to battle though
the other beds and disturb the other bluegill. I always work a bed from
the outside in and disturb the bed as little as possible. Once I catch a
fish, I will work that area real good before I start fishing the center of
the bed," admitted Bill.

Locating Nesting Areas

Whether walking edges of a pond or fishing out of a small jon boat,
my eyes are searching the shallows for bluegill working in water so
shallow that as they move around chasing each other, the water surface
is covered with numerous swirls. If the water is clear and the sun is at
the right angle, it is no trick to see the foot-wide scooped out beds that
look like moon craters. Polarized sunglasses will make it even easier
for you to spot these beds.

Search the shoreline for bluegill working in water so shallow that as they move around chasing each other, the water surface is covered with numerous swirls. These nests are usually in areas exposed to the sun but often in the shade of trees.

Several bluegill nuts that I know locate these spawning beds after dark with a spotlight. The light colored nesting bowl stands out like a sore thumb against the darker bottom.

Look for areas in or around weed beds which contain gravel or sandy bottoms. These nests are usually in areas exposed to the sun but often in the shade of trees. If your lake lacks these bottom elements, hard clay would be the next selection. Masses of dead leaves, pine needles, sticks, and even mud have been selected by these fish as nesting areas. Successful nesting on these sites is very limited.

Many of the beds that you will observe are made by the average-sized bluegill. Expert bluegill chasers fish slightly deeper water to catch the big bulls. While the smaller fish will often be in water as shallow as one foot deep, the shy lunkers I catch seem consistently to come from water three to six feet deep. In clearer waters, I have observed nests underwater at the twenty foot level.

If you are unable to visually locate a spawning area, it is a good idea to simply fish along slowly until you catch three or four fish in quick

This male bluegill guards his nest in the dimly lit waters twenty feet below the surface.

succession. If these fish are males, chances are you have located a bed of bluegills.

Once a bedding site has been found, it is not uncommon that these beds will be good year after year. I have also found that some areas of the same lake will have larger 'gills than others. If your area is loaded with smaller fish, move a short distance down the shoreline and chances are you will find the jumbo fish if your lake is known to have fish of this quality.

Fishing For Spawning Bluegill

Catching bluegill off the beds can be very easy and quite rewarding provided that they use the proper equipment and understand some fishing principles. The clarity of the water, depth of the spawn beds, and velocity and direction of the wind will play an important role in your success.

Undoubtedly the most popular way of fishing for bluegill is with a long slender cane pole, cork, and a hook baited with a worm or brown cricket. This rig is a standard nationwide, but its popularity is at its highest in the south. The length of this pole will vary from ten to eighteen feet.

Cane has been a very popular pole, however, in recent years some excellent fiberglass poles have evolved to take away much of the cane market. However, today anglers can find excellent fiberglass rods to replace the popular cane.

Cane poles, fly rods, and Crappie Stick poles are excellent for spawning bluegill. Note the two poles which are used to position the boat near a spawn bed.

While I enjoy ultralight fishing, long pole fishing will produce more fish per unit of effort. When I do use a cane or fiberglass pole, I like it to be as light and limber as possible. I choose one that will bend almost down to my hand. I always carry one of these poles in my boat because it is impossible at times to reach bluegill that are in brush. You can drop the bait down into any brush pile with a minimum of hang-ups by using this pole.

The pole can be rigged in several different ways. One of the most popular ways in the south is to tie the monofilament to the end of the rod. The length of this line will be one foot shorter than the total length of the pole. Other anglers prefer to have a small reel or line catcher at the base of the pole so additional line can be let out at any time.

When using the fiberglass pole, use a line that is heavy enough to straighten out the small wire hooks. Generally I will use 10 pound clear monofilament in most waters. This will make for faster fishing when you pull the hook loose by straightening it out. You can re-shape the hook with your pliers. Using a lighter line will cause break-offs and lost fishing time when the fish are really hitting. Keep in mind those bull bluegill didn't get that way by being "dumb". When caught, they will make tracks to the brushy structure as fast as a hawg bass. One trick I try if the bluegill takes me into the brush is to give the fish slack line and most of the time it will free itself. Only in very clear waters will I be forced to drop down in line size.

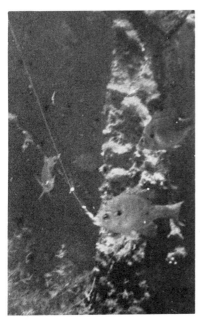

When large hooks are used, the bluegill will steal your bait with such quickness that the hook will never come in contact with the mouth of the bluegill.

A bluegill will rush towards the bait, however, it will pause and study the bait before striking.

Small hooks are the name of the game. This fact was quickly brought to my attention one afternoon while photographing bluegill feeding on crickets and worms which were impaled on a size 2 hook. If you notice, I said feeding and not attempting to feed. These fish would ease up to the bait, study the worm for a few seconds, and then swiftly grab the dangling end of the worm. You set the hook because the bobber went under but the fish wasn't even close to being hooked.

When I had baited the hook with a cricket, the bluegill would approach the bait the same way but the cricket was sucked in with such force that the body of the animal was in pieces. The falling legs, wings, and remaining body parts of the cricket were quickly gobbled up by the remainder of the

BAIT HOOK SIZES

HOOK NUMBERS	HOOK LENGTHS IN INCHES
13/0	4
12/0	3-3/4
11/0	3-1/2
10/0	3-1/4
9/0	3
8/0	2-3/4
7/0	2-1/2
6/0	2-1/4
5/0	2
4/0	1-7/8
3/0	1-3/4
2/0	1-5/8
1/0	1-1/2
1-1/2	1-3/8
1	1-1/4
2	1-1/8
4	15/16
6	13/16
8	11/16
10	9/16
12	7/16
14	11/32
16	9/32
18	7/32
20	5/32

HOOK SIZES ARE DETERMINED BY LENGTH OF SHANK EXCLUDING EYE

Illinois Department of Conservation
Fisheries Division

school. The hook never moved up or down and therefore the bobber would never have moved.

I promptly noted that a Tru-Turn Aberdeen hook in a size 8 or 10 could be buried in the cricket or red wiggler and this offering was sucked into the mouth cavity. The Tru-Turn hook has a unique design which forces the point of the hook to turn into the corner of the bluegill's mouth. The result was a disappearing bobber and another bluegill for the frying pan. Any hook much larger or smaller will present problems.

Also I do not really care to use gold hooks on these fish. Bluegill always ease up to the bait, look it over, and then suck it in. In this meal selecting process, I find that the dark-colored wire hooks are concealed much better in the bait offering than a flashy gold hook.

I have seen many anglers use far to heavy of split shot. Not only can the fish see this, but the heavier shot kills the action of the bait. Use the smallest split shot possible to get the live bait down to the feeding fish. The preferred split shot most anglers seem to use are the removable split shot by Water Gremlin. The Water Gremlin split shot is made by a patented process that forms very soft lead into precise pieces. The result is a controlled hinge which can be squeezed onto the line using your fingers. The Power-Loc jaw grips your line securely with minimum damage to your line. Their famous ears allow you to squeeze the shot off of your line.

The selection of the proper size bobber is critical to taking the fish with any regularity. Most anglers grab the first bobber that they see in a sporting goods store.

When the nest making bulls don't bite during the day in clear water, try fishing for them at dark.

This collection of freshwater shrimp, mayfly nymph, dragon fly nymph, cockroach, and spider by Burke Lures imitate much of the insect life that bluegill feed upon.

This is usually one of the round bobbers that not only damages the mono-filament line, but also offers more resistance in the water. A big bluegill has no trouble in sensing the obstruction on the other end. Small oval slip bobbers, Carbonyte floats, and pencil shaped floats are a much better choice. In a later chapter, the selection and use of bobbers will be discussed.

Tips on Catching Stubborn Jumbo Bluegill

You have been lucky enough to find big bluegill but they won't take your offering. This is a common problem that for many of us can be quite frustrating. In very clear water bedding bluegill can be very spooky of an approaching boat, line and hook, a passing bird overhead, and even your shadow. However, here are a few tips that have worked for me and a few of my friends over the years.

Tip #1. Many of us, when fishing clear water, will make the mistake of using a short fiberglass pole. I have found that if you can use a four-teen to sixteen foot pole and keep the boat anchored as far away from the bed as possible, you will spook fewer fish. I drop down to clear 4 pound test Trilene XL and ahead of that I tie on 2 pound Trilene.

Tip #2. Use the smallest bobber you can buy. Usually the one that you used in ice fishing last winter will work quite nicely. I even slip down to a number 10 wire hook and the smallest slip sinker possible. You will find that a worm will fall into the heart of the bed quite nicely without a piece of split shot but the cricket will float on the surface without the shot.

Tip #3. Feed them what they want. These jumbo fish can be finicky eaters. I like to take along a smorgasbord of live bait. Why not test their appetite with a selection of catalpa worms, red wigglers, brown crickets, grasshoppers, freshwater shrimp, ocean shrimp cut into small pieces, wax worms, and even brown cockroaches. Anyone of these items should turn a fussy bluegill into an eager eater.

Tip #4. When the nest making bulls won't hit during the day in clear water, I sneak back later in the evening or early the next morning. A cloudy or rainy day will prove to be very productive.

Tip #5. If approaching these clear water beds is a real problem, I will even resort to using a fly rod. I will anchor the boat a good dis-tance away from the bed so not to disturb their activity. Eight to ten feet of two pound test leader with a small fly, popping bug, sponge-body black spider, or a tiny spoon will be laid within inches of their bed.

Tip #6. Ultralight jigs and spoons from 1/16 to 1/64 ounce work quite well when used with an ultralight rod and reel. When these tiny jig fall slowly, they imitate much of the insect life that bluegill feed upon. Several baits work quite well in this situation. Try a 1/16 ounce Lindy Fuzz-E-Grub, a Burke Dragon Fly nymph, or Burke Mayfly Nymph as a tempting target. You can also tip these baits with a small piece of worm. Sometimes these fish will strike at a "tipped" jig, yet turn up their noses at a plain jig. Set the hook immediately when the lure is picked up in the nest bed.

CHAPTER 3

How To Fish The Shallows When It's Hot

It doesn't take a lot of angling skill or fishing savvy to catch a boat full of spawning bluegill. However, when they move off the beds it takes an experienced angler to consistently take these summer scrapers.

Many bluegill anglers probably don't take the time to realize that these fish will and do use structure like so many other fish species. These anglers will work the shoreline with red wigglers or popping bugs and "murder" the small 4 inch bluegill and on occasion stumble into a few nice weedbed bluegill.

In this chapter on shallow water fishing, I want you to mentally explore areas and fishing techniques to catch these summer 'gills. All of these areas I have observed underwater while scuba diving and they hold large schools of bream.

Summer Spawn Beds

Many bluegill chasers think only in terms of a May or June spawn. Not so according to many fisheries biologist and fishing guides. Cued by a full moon, a number of these fish will bed all summer long during this moon phase.

Underwater scuba diver, Jay Zapp of Carbondale, Illinois, has pointed this out to me on several occasions. "Three to five days before a full moon the bulls will be actively guarding the nest. The females will shortly follow," said Zapp. "I don't want to leave you with the impression that these beds will have as many bluegills on them as the spring ritual, but a number of these fish are here for the taking."

I was hoping to see this occur as I was writing this book. The May spawn had taken place several months ago when I received a phone call from Joe Sawicki of Carbondale. "I was near a pond yesterday (July 25, 1983) and I noticed a lot of commotion in the shallows. I went over to the area and you won't believe what I saw. There in front of me were seven very large bluegill. Each one of them were guarding a nest. Don't they know that this is July and the temperatures have been running over 100 degrees?" insisted Sawicki.

He checked around the pond and found another area that had three other males on the bed. I checked the calendar and the full moon occurred at 6:35 p.m. on July 24.

When Joe and I met at the spawning bed area at day break on July 29th to fish for them, they were gone. We located them about fifteen feet away in deep water. While we didn't tear them up, we did take over twenty bluegill and two of them tipped the scales at 12 and 16 ounces.

Joe Sawicki with his catch of bluegill taken from deep water near a spawn bed after the full moon on July 29.

With the coming of summer, anglers find little rainfall in there area. This means that the reservoir, farm pond and strip-cut has had the opportunity to clear up. Clearing water makes these summer spawning fish spooky. Anglers must cautiously approach these beds to present live bait or an artificial offering.

Knowledgeable anglers will switch to an ultralight rod and reel spooled with 4 pound test clear monofilament. A clear plastic casting bubble is used to get the mini-jig or live bait near these beds. Early morning or late afternoons are preferred fishing times because the sunlight penetration into the water is minimal thus making it more difficult for the bluegill to become spooked. Fly rod anglers are at an advantage in plucking these fish off the beds.

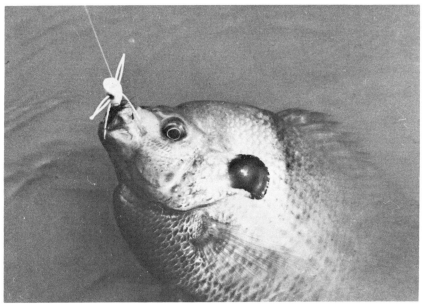

A popping bug laid over the top of a spawning bed triggers an immediate strike.

Boat Docks and Bridges Can Be Red Hot!

Where can you find a mess of bluegill in a hurry? I put this question to Steve Vogts, Zebco's Product Manager for rods. Besides traveling the country for Zebco, Steve also finds time during the year to do some fishing for bluegill. Any angler has to produce for his family and Vogts has certainly zeroed in on these scrappy fish.

Many anglers think that bright light will hurt a bluegill's eyes and that is why bluegill will seek out docks. I doubt this very much. Instead, the bright light hurts a bluegill's sense of security, especially when they are shallow and lack any cover to retreat into.

Structure of a Fish's Eye
(Looking head on at fish's nose)

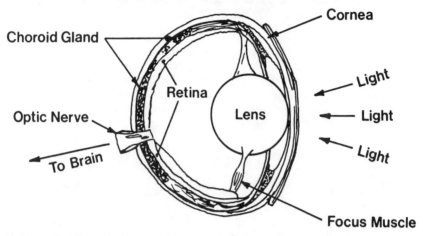

Light passing through the lens of a fish's eye forms an inverted picture on the retina at the back of the eye. This image is transmitted along the optic nerve to the brain.
Drawing courtesy of Berkley and Company.

Many anglers have assumed incorrectly that light hurts a fish's eye since they have no pupil to contract and no eye lid to reduce light intensity. The bluegill's eye can focus on distant objects by retracting an eye muscle which pulls the lens toward the rear of the eye. When the light is bright, the lens is pulled towards the back of the eye and less light falls on it. If light intensities become to high for the fish to adapt, then they can always go deeper, hide under the protective cover of a boat dock, tree, branches, or weeds.

Also the light underwater is never as bright as it is above water. This fact is always true when I dive underwater. I generally have to use a fast color film with an ASA of 400 to get depth of field and film speed. For each foot that you dive, the concentration of light drops off dramatically. Light intensity falls off even more if there would be any particles in the water, an algae bloom at the surface, or a ripple on the surface of the water. It should also be noted that lure color drops off very quickly in the first ten feet of depth.

Some writers have tried to lead anglers into thinking that bluegill take up summer residency under docks because the water is cooler. A quick check of the water temperature with a thermometer will quickly dispel that idea. The simple rule of diffusion demonstrates that if there was cooler water under boat docks, it would quickly mix with the warmer water. Only at depth will you get a stratification of water temperatures, but in the shallows the water temperature will be the same unless a spring is present.

Many bluegill look for security in deep water because it puts a greater distance between them and the surface. The enemies of the bluegill can come into the shallows to feed at any time. This deeper water means that they are less vulnerable to man and other predators. If the lake lacks deep water with structure, then the docks will provide the security blanket for these fish. They may become edgy but they will be content to live here most of the summer even though a number of them will fall victim to man and the black bass.

Vogts has discovered a technique of fishing docks which is so successful that it keeps his freezer full of fish. However, Steve doesn't fish just any dock in this Spirit Lake area. He is very selective in looking for docks which lie very close to the surface of the water. He finds that these docks need to be less than a foot from the water surface. The lower docks afford more prolonged shade through out the day and therefore they are much more attractive to bluegill. Any dock that sits high over the water will dissipate the shade.

"Boat docks that are located in 5 to 12 feet of water are the first place that I fish during the heat of the summer," revealed Vogts. "These docks are extremely attractive to bluegill because they provide shade and food. The dock pilings are covered with moss which hide a number of aquatic organisms upon which these bluegill love to feed. Small freshwater shrimp, newly hatched minnows, small crappie, perch, and bluegill are relished by the larger bluegill."

Look for docks which are close to the surface of the water near deep water and have underwater weeds growing under and around them. Look for brush piles within six to eight feet of a dock.

"I look for the flat-top docks which have underwater weeds growing under and around them," said Steve. He went on to say, "The better docks are going to have some age to them. The longer the dock has been in the water, the better the chance the bluegills will have to form an association with it. Any new dock seldom draws any amount of fish. It may take several years to become a productive fishing site.

Vogts also looks for docks that are near deep water. Bluegill can retreat into this water anytime that a large predator fish goes on the prowl.

"Finding these docks is one thing, fishing them is another," disclosed Steve. He prefers to use a five to five and one half foot ultralight spinning rod, 4 pound Trilene XL line, and extremely small jigs.

When Steve says a small jig, he isn't kidding. He suggests anglers using 1/64 to 1/32 ounce jigs. Steve has found through experimentation that there are two basic color patterns. The two colors he recommends is a yellow hair jig or a mini-jig with a black body and chartreuse curly-tail. When fishing is really tough, he tips the bait with a wasp larvae or wax worm.

His technique is to back off approximately 20 feet from the dock and skip the jig under the dock. This means that the angler has to use a sidearm presentation to get the bait to skip under the dock. He constantly watches for a slight twitch in his light line. Glass polaroids are a must for seeing the fish.

This dock is located too high above the surface of the water and very few bass and bluegill are found here.

Steve will catch 20 to 30 bluegill from under these docks. Over the years, he has learned that the larger bluegill will be found within a foot of the bottom. Getting your lure down through the smaller fish to the jumbo bream is not easy.

After taking up to 30 fish, he will motor to another uock and repeat the process. He usually returns to his best docks later in the afternoon. However, he will not necessarily throw his jig under the dock this time. The shade of the dock will not be under it, but to the side of it. He will then cast to this shaded area and continues putting more bluegill into his ice chest.

Are some days better than others for this type of fishing? "You bet!" said Vogts. "I look for hot days with bright, high skies, no wind, and very muggy conditions. Just remember that at high noon these fish are directly under the dock but later in the day they will be off to the side of this structure. My preferred time of the day is one to four o'clock in the afternoon."

Steve just doesn't catch bluegill with his technique. He will put bass, crappie, catfish, walleye, and perch on his stringer.

When your favorite docks have had a large number of bluegill taken from beneath them, why not try the bridges or railroad trestle on your lake?

Fishing for bluegill under and around a heavily traveled bridge can supply plenty of action. Each year a number of anglers will ask me where they can catch lots of fish. The answer I give them is docks and bridges. The steady hum of traffic going on overhead seems to be of no hindrance to these fish. Dozens of knowledgeable anglers consistently fill their stringers in these areas.

Bridges are artificially built structures of concrete and rocks. They generally have a deep channel running under them which provides the area with a constant flow of aerated water. Shade is found in abundance. The concrete or wooden pilars are covered with algae which attract aquatic insects, shad, and small minnows.

A few of Bob Folder's panfish lures. Shown from left to right is the panfish popper, black water bug, wooly worm, peacock wooly, beetle fly, and black ant.

A bridge is a bottleneck because it narrows down a section of the lake. This means that baitfish and other forage organisms, which are passing the area, will have to use the channel passage under the bridge as a means of getting from one side to the other. In other words, a bridge is a concentrator of food.

Worms, crickets, tiny jigs, flies, Deep Teeny Crawfish, and Beetle-Spins are very good bait choices. Many anglers will use small bobbers with their live bait and jigs.

Some very nice panfish poppers, water bugs, wooly worms, flies, and nymphs are made by Bob Folder Lures, R.R. 2, Hazlett Lane, Springfield, Illinois 62707. These small lures can be fished with a slip-bobber, clear casting bobber, or a fly rod. These folks have some excellent colored jigs and they aren't your run of the mill ten cent jigs.

Spoon feed a bluegill? You bet I do. A spoon can be effectively jigged vertically alongside pilings and boat docks. Keep the spoon close to the pilings and give it a quivering action with your rod tip all the way to the bottom as it falls. This tight line fishing will allow you to feel even a very light strike. Most of these bluegill will eagerly grab the fluttering spoon as an easy meal or because of competition from other bluegill in the school.

When jigging these ice fly spoons vertically, it doesn't hurt to add a piece of red wiggler, meal worm, or maggot to the small hook. Even a small ball of bread on the hook can be effective.

The largest selection of ice fly spoons can be obtained from Comet Tackle, 2794 Midway Street, Uniontown, Ohio 44685. These baits retail for about forty cents per spoon. Comet Tackle has eleven styles of ice

Comet Tackle's nymph, ice fly spoons and black ants, Codell's cottontail spinner, Mr. Twister single spin, Mr. Twister jig, and a Lindy Fuzz-E-Grub are excellent baits to be fished around docks and pilings.

flies in ten different colors. These small spoons are a work of art and they are great for ice fishing.

All of these baits should be first fished around the pilings. The depth will have to be varied to find the feeding fish. Extreme care should be taken not to bump the pilings if you are fishing from a boat. This will move the fish away from this structure. Excessive outboard noise should also be avoided.

Another method of fishing these pilings was a tip passed onto me by Tom Mann. Tom's advice was for fishing crappie, however, I have found that it works quite well for bluegill.

Tom's method is basically quite simple. He eases his boat next to the bridge abutment or piling, and switches on his depth finder. Tom indicated that the depth finder is important during the day since fish will vary their depth. He readily locates fish on his flasher.

He backs away from the bridge about ten to twelve yards and casts parallel to the pilings. He throws past the pilings and letting the small jig drift down into their feeding zone.

Mann uses the count down method of fishing. Since he likes to throw 1/32 ounce jigs or smaller, he keeps track of his count until he makes contact with a fish. Once a fish is caught he continues to use that count to catch his fish. He moves from one piling to another catching fish.

The method described above is not only great on crappie but you will soon learn that it will take more than your share of bluegill.

After successfully fishing the pilings, begin working the rip-rap corners of the bridge. Cast parallel to the shore. Start the lure shallow and gradually work the bait deeper and further away from the shoreline.

Cold Fronts and Bluegill Fishing

It was my first trip to the famous Reelfoot Lake in northwestern Tennessee. Even though spawning was late that year, these fish were starting to bed in earnest. A cold front followed me all the way down from Illinois leaving Reelfoot with high blue skies and a chilly northwest wind. It turned these fish off the feed bag just as though they were largemouth bass. Guide Bennie Smith worked very hard for the both of us to come up with close to 30 quality bream.

No one travels more than Bill Dance. He loves to fish for anything that swims. When I asked Bill how a cold front affects these fish, he had some very interesting ideas.

"Barometric pressure changes affect any species of animal," said Dance. "I think bluegill are even more sensitive to the pressure changes of a cold front than are bass. During the summer months, a bluegill doesn't go extremely deep. Ten or fifteen feet is probably maximum. However, some bass may drop thirty or forty feet. Deep fish are more predictable fish as the result of weather changes whether it be summer or winter. A drastic pressure change will not affect deep fish as much as it will these shallower living bluegill."

Dance went on to say that as a big weather change is moving into an area bluegill will turn into a feeding frenzy. "However, as a big high pressure comes in behind this storm, it will turn them off. In the summer months, the fronts are not that severe and the bluegill will go back to feeding in two or three days," disclosed Bill.

"You know what I think happens to these fish?" asked Dance. "I think it affects their equilibrium and therefore they just aren't in the mood to feed. I think pressure affects every living creature and this will affect their behavior."

"I know it is going to be very tough fishing for these inactive blue-

When a cold front moves into an area, big bluegill can still be caught but it will take more skill and patience.   Photo by Kris Wunderle

gill," said Dance. "I like to spray a fish attractor like Fish Formula II on my bait to stimulate them into feeding."

"Recently, I was fishing on Reelfoot when a cold front hit the area. A good friend of mine, Al Hamilton, had joined me to fish for bluegill. They wouldn't hit any crickets, worms, or lures. I could see them bubbling. We would put our offering within inches of them but we had no takers. I sprayed some Fish Formula II on my cricket and I immediately started picking up bream," confessed Dance.

In chapter 6, I will discuss chemical fish attractors and how they might be able to stimulate your inactive bluegill into feeding. It just may mean more fish on your stringer.

CHAPTER 4

Deep Water Fishing For Summer Bluegill

If you are fishing a strange lake, then it is very important to get a map and look for areas that should hold concentrations of fish. Knowledgeable anglers will start a systematic search pattern for summer bluegill. The summer spawn beds are checked if it is a full moon, next the boat docks and pilings, and if finding no action, the last two areas to search are the weedlines next to deep water and finally deep water structure.

Fish The Edges of Cover Near Deep Water

"Fish the edges of cover near any deep water for bluegill in the summer," advised Tony Dean, outdoor writer and broadcaster for In-Fisherman radio. Tony fishes the northern lakes for a variety of species. "Cover can be anything from a boat dock, pier, underwater brush pile, or the edge of a thick weed bed," said Dean.

"After the spawning ritual, one of the first post-spawn areas they retreat to is the nearest drop-off. If the lake or pond is dishpan shaped and has no drop-off, look for them along the deep water sides of weed beds. In shallow ponds and lakes, the larger fish will remain along the outside edges of dense weeds. The smaller bluegill will be found along the inside edges of the weedline," Tony revealed.

In most of our lakes, aquatic vegetation fulfills three important requirements: cover, food production, and dissolved oxygen.

All bluegill instinctively seek cover as an escape from predators. These weeds offer an important source of cover for baitfish and maturing bluegill.

The bulk of food production occurs where water weeds are found. Insects, small minnows, crustaceans, and other small fishes are found feeding and living here. It is an underwater buffet for growing and mature bluegill.

There are times during the summer when low levels of dissolved oxygen are found in our lakes. When this occurs, these fish migrate to the weedline for their oxygen requirements. It is easy to understand why at some times of the year many species of gamefish will join the bluegill in the weedline.

Tony Dean went on to tell me that water clarity will determine how deep these fish will suspend. "It is not uncommon to find bluegill in stained water not much deeper than 5 or 6 feet deep all summer long with movements into shallow water during low light periods. However, in clearer lakes where there is more sunlight penetrating into the water, you are talking about deeper water bluegills," disclosed Dean.

A good pair of Red Ball waders and a spincast reel loaded with four pound test line will let you fish near deep water where the jumbo bluegill hang out. 　　　　　　　　　　　　　Photo by Bill Sargent

How do you get to these deep water bluegill? Tony puts his fly rod away and picks up his spinning tackle with clear four pound test line. He will use the clear plastic casting bubble to get his small weighted fly down to these fish. He will rarely utilize live bait unless a cold front comes into his area. Then he finds that a worm or cricket really will do a number on these deeper fish.

Tony will fill his clear plastic bubble with a small amount of water so it will sink very slowly. He then ties his hook, baited with a worm or cricket, about two feet ahead of the bubble. In very clear water, he will place the bubble three to four feet behind the baited hook which will make casting more difficult.

Nymphs and popping bugs can be fished over spawning beds in very clear water by using a clear plastic bubble two to three feet ahead of these baits.

"The key to catching these bluegill is to move the bait very slowly and fish the bait parallel to the weedline," said Dean. He went on to tell me that the best action to catch these fish is "little teeny pauses and twitches" moving the fly or live bait no more than an inch at a time. They rarely hit the bait as it is moving but instead they will smack the lure on the pause.

If the bluegill aren't too deep, Tony likes to use a black sponge-rubber spider. To make the spider sink, he will pinch the rubber body under the water so the sponge will soak up the liquid. It will sink quicker on the cast. Tony warns that your line must have no slack because these fish will suck in the offering and spit it out. With a slack line, the angler would never be able to feel the strike. A sharp hook is very critical in hooking these fish.

Another lure that has been quite effective for me has been the Mepps spinners. A plain number 0 or 1 Mepps Aglia, Black Fury, or single hook Comet will trigger plenty of action. Tipping this spinner with a small piece of worm will at times make it even better.

The Aglia style blade is the original Mepps spinner. The blade revolves at about a 60 degree angle from the spinner body. The nice feature about this spinner is that the blade will spin at very slow retrieves which makes it very attractive to non-aggressive bluegill.

In early morning, at dusk or in overcast weather, it only takes a little flash or movement to start bluegill into a feeding mood. Too much flash, and these fish will back off from your lure. Mepps recently introduced the "red hot fury" which has fluorescent red dots on the spinner blade. This lure is very effective during low light visibility, murky water, or heavy overcast conditions.

My good friend Joe Hughes of Rebel Lures loves to fish the "lay down trees" near islands or shoreline. Big bream will be found near this structure. Joe likes live bait as well as anyone, however, he loves to fish a tiny crawfish crankbait near this cover. Rebel's Deep Teeny Crawfish, when fished on an ultralight rod and reel, is quite lethal. Joe prefers to use 6 pound test monofilament line or less when casting for these fish. He uses a technique of casting, retrieving, stopping, and twitching the lure. Generally, the bluegill will smack the crawfish when it stops.

Rebel's Deep Teeny Crawfish, when fished with an ultralight rod and reel, is lethal on jumbo bluegill.

I have found this lure is tough to beat when you need some bluegill in a hurry. In some states, you can use live bream for striper bait.

You can throw this lure along any shoreline and have enough striper bait to last you all day. This bait maybe small, but it will take its share of bass, crappie, walleye, catfish, and even other game species. It should be a part of any tackle box.

Fish Deep Water Breaklines

If you have fished the weedlines, docks, piers, and shallow brush piles but found they were not hitting, then you should next look to the deeper water. Many anglers will say that they are fishing deeper water, which is true. However, they are not concentrating their fishing efforts on the structure which is found on the deep water drop-offs. The home of many fish species is deep water and big fish will remain in these areas all day. In the evening hours they swim slowly to the shallower areas to feed.

Many of us will fish a variety of ponds, lakes, oxbows, and streams for the tasty fish. However, to tell you to fish deep in small ponds would be wrong. A scientific study by I.B. Byrd of the Alabama Department of Conservation demonstrated where bluegill go in the summer. Byrd set out to show the depth distribution of bluegill in farm ponds. He trapped bluegill with 1-inch or 1/4 inch mesh wire traps which were equipped with two internal funnels. He set the traps at various depths from 2 to 9 feet in a 2-acre pond and from 4 to 8 feet in a 22-acre pond. Depths of 4.5 to 8 feet were trapped in the 3, 6, and 26 acre ponds. His traps were lifted and the fish removed either once or twice daily, but occasionally they were checked every two days. Water samples were collected from the various depths and analyzed for dissolved oxygen and carbon dioxide.

The results of his study were most interesting. The critical depth at which bluegill could live was normally 5 feet in the 2-acre pond and 7 feet in the 22-acre pond during the period of summer stratification. This study was conducted during the period from June 24 through September 12. He found the bluegill in the shallower water. He noted that they were unable to live in the deep water longer than 6 to 45 hours where the dissolved oxygen was at a very low 0.3 parts per million and a carbon dioxide concentration of 4.4 parts per million or more.

With increases in the surface areas of the pond from 2 to 22-acres, the critical depths increased apparently as the result of deeper mixing of the waters due to increased wave action. The critical depth at which these fish could live increased in all ponds following strong winds, heavy rainfalls, or cool periods. This depth decreased during periods of extended cloudiness or other conditions resulting in reduced photosynthetic activity in the deeper waters.

A larger body of water will provide a greater depth of oxygenated water for these fish to reside. Found within these reservoirs will be many points with long, gently slanting slopes that ease into deeper depths. On the underwater points will be found brush, trees, rock piles,

On the underwater points will be found brush, trees, rock piles, weedbeds, and other structure which will attract big bluegill.

weedbeds, and other structure which will attract bluegill. Such areas are more productive than the sharp, steep vertical drop-offs.

The above statement has been proven to be a true fact on every underwater dive that I have been on during the summer months. One hot July day I slipped below the placid water of my favorite diving lake. Small bluegills rushed into to investigate the disturbance in their territory. After feeding a few of them red wigglers from our hands, my diving partner and I eased toward a dock which had the planking close to the top of the water. Small to medium sized bluegill could be observed scattered under the dock and each one looking for a free meal.

Where were the jumbo 'gills? I remembered an old wharf near by which had rotted and slipped quietly into the low light depth of a twenty foot drop-off. We eased into the bone chilling water of the thermocline and quickly discovered big bluegill heaven. All around us were jumbo bream in the 12-14 ounce weight class. No small fish were with this exclusive big fish school. These fish could have been easily caught if the local anglers would have known the exact location of the moss-covered wharf.

With less than one half of a tank of air left, we swam to a vertical cliff area twenty five yards away. Here we found a few very small bluegill and bass but no large bream could be found anywhere. This summer pattern exists every time I swim in these lakes.

Swimming with any fish species on their terms is a very exhilarating and educational experience. Fishing deep for the big bream is a lesson not to be forgotten. The second lesson is fishing the right bait or lure. Your fishing technique should not be neglected either.

Small boats work well on small ponds and lakes. This folding Porta-Bote is perfect for strapping to the top of your car or camping trailer. Since it is made out of space-age material, it won't sink.

A summer fishing pattern started to emerge. Fish deep, fish slow, and use lures that will imitate small flies and underwater nymphs, but how in the world do you get those small nymphs down to their level?

To my rescue came an idea from my brother Terry. Terry probably is one of the most knowledgeable anglers that you could share a boat with. Also on Terry's side, is one of the finest set of fish sensitive hands that you could inherit. If a crappie or bluegill so much as breathes on his lure, it is as good as being in the cooler.

Terry loves to use his short ice-fishing rod in the heat of the summer for panfish. He adds a stainless steel wire to his rod tip which gives him extra sensitivity for his technique which involves a combination of ideas. This product is called a Spring Bobber which can be slipped on your rod near the tip. It sells for about $1.50 and is manufactured by Schooley's, Greenville, Michigan.

He likes using very small flies or nymphs on deep water drops. Getting light flies or nymphs down into their deep water dining room is no problem for him.

Tied to his ultralight spincasting reel is found 4 pound clear Trilene XL. To this he ties a five foot length of one or two pound test leader. To the bottom of the leader he ties a weighted 1/8 ounce plastic jig or small ice fishing spoon. Nine inches above this he ties a 1/2-inch dropper loop which sticks out at a right angle to the leader. To this dropper loop he ties on a fly or nymph with two inches of two pound test line. Six to eight inches above this he ties in another fly or nymph of a different color. He prefers to use flies or nymphs in a size No. 10 to 16.

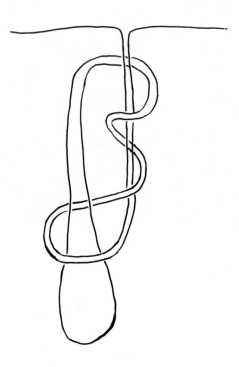

A number of dropper knots are tied, but this one is the most dependable with a 63 percent reliability. The other two dropper knots tested had a reliability of only 43 and 50 percent, respectively.

"You need to have a very delicate touch to feel these fish nipping at your lure," said Terry. He lowers his rig to the bottom, reels in the slack line, and twitches the rod tip up and down. His rod tip moves no more than one inch while he gradually raises his forearm and rod. It may take him 20 to 40 seconds to raise his rod tip from waist level to slightly above his head.

"This quivering action of the lure imitates the action of a variety of small aquatic organisms, especially nymphs swimming to the surface. I use a variety of colors to duplicate the organism they are feeding upon," revealed Terry.

Another trick he uses in the summer is cut up saltwater shrimp. He cuts the frozen shrimp up into 1/4 - 3/8 inch pieces and buries a short shanked No. 8 or 10 hook into the pieces. The head, tail, and shell of the snrimp is thrown into the water as chum. The baited shrimp is fished tight line or with a slip-bobber with great success. On real picky bluegill I have even known him to color his clear monofilament line with a permanent felt tip marker every six inches for additional camouflage.

I have found that a Lindy Floating Rig to be a new approach for deep water bluegill. Back in the early 1960's the Lindner brothers revolutionized live bait fishing with a rig that puts a sliding lead weight down on the bottom where the fish are located. A worm, minnow, or leech is then

A Lindy Floating Rig is a new approach for deep water bluegill. A worm hooked into a small short shanked hook is very attractive to these deep water fish.

Drawing by Steve Bradley.

hooked into a small short shanked hook. The floating rig has gone one step further by adding a depth adjustable urethane float. Now your worm or cricket is kept free of fish discouraging weeds and muck that can make live bait totally unproductive. Your live bait remains alive and frisky longer and most live bait will fight the float for even greater fish enticing action.

For suspended fish, let the sinker rest on the bottom and feed line cut through the sinker which lets your bait float into the fish zone. Your boat should be stationary or barely moving if you are going to use this method. It works quite well when I am bank fishing and the bait needs to be in deeper water.

Terry uses one additional trick when he locates a school of nice bluegill. He takes along a quart-size Chlorox bottle with the cap sealed to the bottle. He ties 20 to 30 feet of light monofilament line to the plastic bottle and a one half pound sinker to the opposite end. As he drifts along the drop-off watching his Lowrance portable depth finder, he is careful to note any fish below. When he spots a school, he slips the bottle into the water to mark the spot of the school. He quietly hovers over the area using his dropper fly-nymph technique of fishing.

In order to find these fish, Terry relies upon a depth finder. "Don't get me wrong," said Terry, "you don't have to spend money on a depth finder to locate bluegill, but it sure helps when they go deep. I particularly like the depth finders that are portable and run off lantern batteries. These units are very good in locating bluegill on a frozen lake."

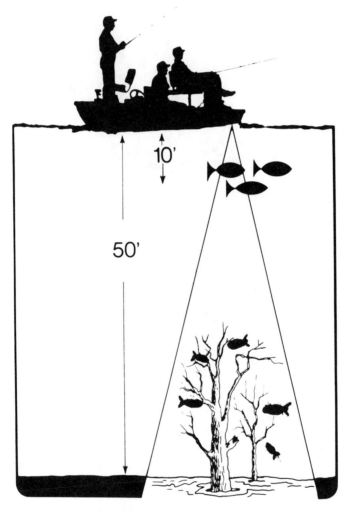

A portable depth finder in deep water will help anglers locate brush filled with bluegill. Drawing furnished by Lowrance Electronics.

CHAPTER 5

Ultralight Fishing Techniques That Catch More Bluegill

The objective of this book is for you to become the most successful angler in your area. However, locating fish, knowing what baits to use and how to use them play only a part of your total game plan. Rods, reels, hooks, bobbers, fishing knots, and lines are seldom thought about when attempting to catch bluegill. None of these tackle items are created equally. I personally want you to become the best at what you like doing, catching bluegill, therefore this chapter takes a hard look in detail at overcoming your tackle problems.

Rods and Reels

The selection of a rod and reel is one of the most important decisions an angler can make. Whether you are an ardent bluegill chaser or only a weekend warrior, proper equipment is important when going after any fish species.

Many anglers get by quite nicely by using just an old cane pole. For me to change their successful fishing method would be wrong. Many of the old timers have converted to the newer graphite pole such as the Crappie Stick. It is tough to make a graphite pole with the resilient, fast and delicate touch of a cane pole, but these folks did it. They accomplished this by using a two-part construction which allows them to make a long, light weight, but strong pole. Their pole retains the necessary backbone to do a real job on bream and crappie all day long. They make these poles in lengths ranging from 8½ to 14 feet. These great poles are made of a composite for strength and sensitivity. Zebco makes their longest 14 foot pole in a telescopic model that only weighs eight ounces. Their series of nine Crappie Stick rods are designed to give crappie anglers a set of matched rods to meet almost any fishing situation.

You can catch bluegill with cheap, poorly matched equipment. But with all the headaches of poor casting and snarled lines inside your reels, you will soon agree that you have not had a very enjoyable experience.

Spincasting is probably the easiest to learn for the beginning angler. These "push-button" reels are mounted on top of the rod and can be matched to any rod designed for baitcasting. The nice feature about these reels is that they do not backlash, but some are noted for line twisting.

They are relatively trouble free so long as you use the right line size for that reel. If the reel can only handle up to 8 pound test, don't try and squeeze even a small line diameter 12 pound test on the reel. Anglers that want to cast ultra small jigs will have to use 2-4 pound test line to

A spincast reel spooled with four pound test line can be just as effective in taking large bream as a cane pole.
Photo by Bill Sargent

accomplish their objective. Eight to ten pound test line with small baits might go 6 feet if you are lucky. Match the line size to the lure.

Casting with the spincasting system is very easy. Simply push the button with your thumb and hold it until it's time to release the bait during the forward cast.

When selecting a spincasting reel, I look for several features. A smooth drag is very important in playing a fish. A drag which sticks when fighting a fish will cost you not only the bluegill but also time that you could have spent catching other fish. One of the finest drag systems is found on the Zebco CR60 Crappie Classic spincast reel. Also this reel has a specially designed pickup system which tracks the line back every time into your reel after a cast. Some spincast reels don't always do this and key strikes are missed.

Any drag that sticks when using even the best premium monofilament will cause line failure. Remember that sand or dirt in a reel will destroy the operation of the drag. If this debris gets into your reel, you should clean it immediately.

Another reel at your sporting goods dealer is the Ryobi spincast reel. One nice feature of the Ryobi spincast reel is the no-line-twist feature. Many beginning anglers when playing a fish will continue reeling their line even though the fish hasn't moved an inch. This continual reeling will twist the line so badly in most reels that you will have great difficulty in making future casts. You can't twist line with the Ryobi.

You probably won't be able to cast light lures as far with the spincast rod and reel as you could with a spinning outfit, but the spincast system will allow you to skip small jigs under boat docks for those hard to catch summer bluegill.

What spincast rod should an angler look for? I asked John Scott, Public Relations Manager for Zebco, that question. "From my personal experience and in talking with other successful bluegill chasers, I would recommend a light-medium action five foot to five foot six inch rod. For many fishermen a fiberglass rod will do just fine, however, more experienced bluegill anglers will probably prefer a light-medium action rod of graphite composite." Scott said.

Spinning reels are basically trouble free and very light lures can be thrown into a brisk wind. The line very smoothly peels off these reels with very little friction.

Most fishing manuals demonstrate holding the line under the index finger before casting. When the forward cast is made, the line is released. Sounds good on paper but most of the time the line catches on the index finger and your lure goes about two feet. Next time you cast with this reel, control your line by holding it with the right forefinger against the rod. Now open the bail with your left hand. From this point on your casting method differs. Pinch the monofilament against the front of the reel spool with your left forefinger. Cast the reel with your right arm but feather the line as it comes off the spool with your left forefinger. It is very different from what you have been taught but it works.

One of the standards in spinning reels has been the Garcia Cardinal series. Their Cardinal 752 ultralight reel has a self-centering bail which puts the line at your finger tips. Also found is a very smooth rear drag system which is numerically calibrated. Other features include a push button spool for easy conversion from one line weight to another and an oscillating spool which stores the line in parallel rows for those long casts. It holds 2-6 pound test line.

Another nice hybrid spinning reel with its ultra smooth drag system is the Zebco Omega 144. This trigger reel system comes spooled with 60 yards of 6 pound test Trilene line. A five to six foot glass or graphite light-medium action rod would be a perfect match for this reel.

Many anglers love to search out bluegill with a fly rod. One of the greatest fly rodders of all time is Bernard "Lefty" Kreh of Cockeyville, Maryland. Lefty is one of the premier outdoor writers in the United States. He loves to fish for anything that swims. Recently, upon returning from a deep sea fishing trip, Lefty was on the phone the very next day coaxing a friend into going fly fishing for bluegill. If you love to fish, you understand the reason why.

When I needed material for this book on fly fishing for bluegill, their was only one person to turn to, and that was Lefty. The following tips come from years of experience.

One of the greatest fly rodders of all time, "Lefty" Kreh, intently studies a deep water area on one of his favorite streams.

Photo by Barbara Lewis

"The best fly rods are nine footers," said Kreh. "The longer fly rod allows me to manipulate the fly better, lift more line from the water when you are wadding deep and it is more forgiving on the cast. The best fly rods will handle four through seven line size."

"If I had to select one fly rod and line combination, I'd go for the weight forward floater six line, unless I was fishing in deeper lakes. The seven weight comes in handy when you fish depths of more than four feet (deep water farm ponds and clear lakes). Here a sinking fly line or a sinking tip line will work better than a floater most of the time," said Kreh as he was meticulously tying his favorite bluegill nymph.

Lefty likes to use an unweighted fly on a long leader and a floating line when the bluegill are on the spawn beds. Lefty said, "When you put that fly into the spawning area it is like rolling a wine bottle into a jail cell — you'll get an argument trying to get it back."

An unweighted fly, a long leader, and a floating line will take a large number of bluegill off the spawn beds.   Photo by Bill Sargent

Kreh told me that some of the best fly rodding can be found wadding small streams in the east and mid-west which hold millions of these scrappy fish. A tiny, sleek popper with almost no dressing (only a short tail that cannot foul on the cast) works best. "On streams I work the bug constantly to give the bluegill the impression that here is a struggling, living, helpless insect," indicated Kreh.

What is the most important fly fishing tip you can give anglers? Lefty answered my question faster than a speeding fly line. "I think the most important factor in retrieve is that the fly or bug, on or below the surface, should never appear to be aggressive. The bluegill is a small fish, and I find that bugs or wet flies and streamers that work to fast or aggressively, apparently make the bluegill wonder if they should really tackle the fly."

Kreh went on to tell me that color sometimes makes a difference. "If basic nymphs are brown, then brown wet flies and nymphs will usually do better. However, I find that almost everywhere wet flies with a chenille body of florescent chartreuse appeal to bluegills very well."

Lefty feels that it is important to have flies of the same pattern that are unweighted, lightly weighted and heavily weighted. There will be situations where one or the other of these lures will get to the fish better.

Sharp Anglers Use Sharp Hooks

It may come as a great shock to many of us but the difference between hooking and not hooking a fish is less than one thousandth of an inch.

Virtually all hooks when purchased in a box or on a lure are DULL! Yet, many of us simply ignore this fact in our hurry to get out on the lake. This simple mistake costs us more fish each year than we would like to think.

One individual in this country has spent considerable time investigating how hooks should be sharpened to catch more fish. Paul Johnson of Berkley and Company has researched this problem which took him to a leading manufacturer of fish hooks. They could not give a satisfactory definition of a sharp hook. He finally contacted Davis and Geck Division of American Cyanamid. This company has a team of scientist that study sharpness in suture needles for various tissues.

Johnson indicated that he thought that "a perfectly round, sewing needle point might be the ideal hook point". However, he soon discovered that such a point was not only difficult to sharpen, but the end result was the removal of too much metal, which caused a weak point. He also realized that a dull hook would require a lot of pressure to adequately set the hook for any fish species. He knew he had to find another solution for creating a sharp hook.

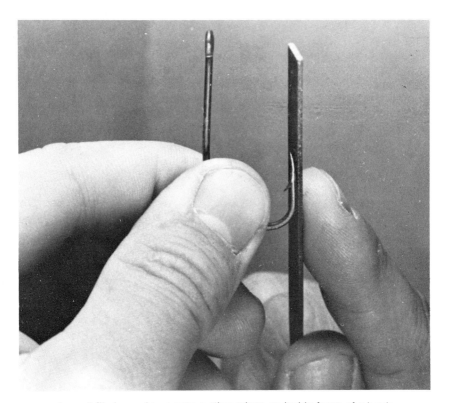

A small file is used to create cutting edges on inside faces of a hook.
Photo courtesy of Berkley and Company

Using a fine jeweler's file and a 180 grit carborundum paper, he could approach the hook sharpness desired. He was able to stroke sharp edges running from the barb to the point. A two-edged oval point profile was formed using the carborundum paper. His end results almost matched the medical suture needle design called the "side-cutting-spatula". You can achieve similar results by obtaining a small bastard mill file from the hardware store or purchase one of the diamond hook files made by EZE-LAP.

His research demonstrated that used, dull hooks required penetration forces as much as three times higher than factory new hooks. When he measured the hook penetrating force in the mouth of a bluegill, he discovered that a dull hook took about 1 1/2 pounds of force. A factory new hook required about 3/4 of a pound of hook setting force. His hand sharpened SCS hook took only 1/2 pound of force to be embedded in the mouth of the bluegill. This represents quite a difference when you are attempting to catch hook-smart bluegill on light line.

Is your hook dull? Try the simple test of drawing the point of your hook across your thumbnail without stopping. A sharp hook not only will leave a light scratch across the fingernail but it will try to dig into the nail. A dull hook "skates" down your nail.

How To Set Your Reel's Drag

Less than ten anglers out of 100 know how to adjust and use their fishing reel's drag mechanism. Maybe it's because the basic principle looks simple, or perhaps because there has been a notable lack of information made available to help educate fisherman. More fish are lost and more blame placed on bad line or lack of fishing skill, when in fact the true cause may be failure to properly use the reel's drag control.

Fishermen know there is an incredible variety of reels being sold, each of which uses different variations of a line drag control. These designs all share one common objective: to provide a slippage mechanism which will permit line to be stripped from the spool at a lower force than that required to break the line.

Common practice has been to start out a morning's fishing by first giving a few tugs on the line. If the line strips off the reel without poppin', everything's OK. Sound familiar?

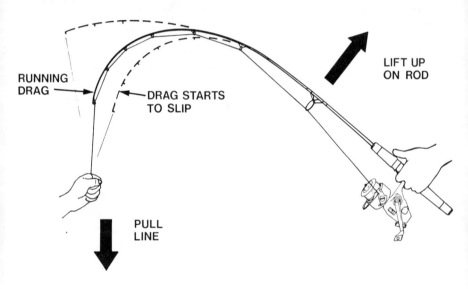

Proper Way To Set A Reel Drag

The drag on a reel must be set properly, especially when using very light lines.

Drawing courtesy of Berkley and Company

A better way to check for drag adjustment is to thread the line through the rod guides of the rod. Tests show the length of the rod, its stiffness, and the number of guides all can affect drag performance. Now, have your buddy pull on the line while you flex the rod and apply line tension in the normal fishing mode. Adjust the drag to the point where line can be stripped without breaking when you rare back as if to set the hook.

Observe the tip of the rod. Does it bounce erratically as line is stripped off the slipping drag? If so, you might have a dry, dirty drag mechanism that could use a cleaning and spray shot of silicone. You may notice that the tip of the rod bends farther down at first until the drag starts working.

Lab tests have proven that almost all fishing reels have drags which have an erratic stick-slip character. The cheaper the reel, the more the problem. The initial force required to break this static sticking may run several pounds higher than the lower running drag once line is peeling off the reel. Keep this in mind when setting the drag and back off drag pressure a few notches to compensate for this slip-stick behavior.

Keep the reel spool filled. The mechanical advantage exerted on the drag mechanism drops as the spool diameter decreases.

When you fish with the popular ultra-light lines, be extra careful in setting your reel's drag. A judgement error that adds one to two extra pounds drag force when using a heavier pound test mono may not be critical, but apply this to a situation when using four pound test monofilament and it will be disastrous.

All Bobbers Are Not Created Equally

The basic idea behind a float is for the angler to control the depth of their bait. All bobbers will do this. However, a bobber really needs to do much more than this for you to become successful.

If you really stop and think, you want a bobber that won't cause a picky bluegill to drop your bait, but yet one that is sensitive enough to tell you that your bait is lively and very attractive to the fish.

Recently, I evaluated four different styles of bobbers. The four bobbers chosen were the familiar round bobber, the pencil-shaped bobber with a spring at the top, Lindy slip bobber, and the Carbonyte float. The Carbonyte float is a British float which has been introduced into this country only in recent years.

Small diameter monofilament lines are easily damaged by line nicks and abrasions. Since bobbers and slip sinkers are just one more addition to your fishing line which could cause monofilament damage, I wanted to know how each one of these bobbers would affect your line.

I used 12 pound test Trilene XL which had been soaked in lake water for four hours. A total of 25 line tests were made on each bobber. The line was tested on a professional line testing machine which was loaned to me by Berkley and Company of Spirit Lake, Iowa.

The monofilament line strength averaged 13.18 pounds without any bobbers in the system. However, as soon as I started adding the different bobbers to the system, small line weaknesses could be seen.

The popular red and white round bobber was tested first. The line broke at 11.7 pounds leaving only 89 percent of the line strength. The

Lindy slip bobber had 97 percent (12.8 pound average break strength) of its line strength left after line failure. The pencil-shaped, balsa wood fishing float also showed 97 percent line reliability with the monofilament line breaking at an average of 12.8 pounds. The Carbonyte fishing float had an average line breakage of 12.92 (98 percent reliability).

The round red and white snap-on bobbers are the most frequently used bobbers by bluegill anglers, but they have several drawbacks. These bobbers do damage the line but more important they offer a greater amount of resistance in the water. This means that the picky eating jumbo bluegill can and do feel resistance when taking the bait. A small bluegill may not even be able to pull the bobber under the water's surface.

The Lindy slip bobber rig is quite easy to use. A dacron tie is tied directly to the monofilament line at the depth you want to fish. There are no beads, plastic sleeves or springs to worry about.

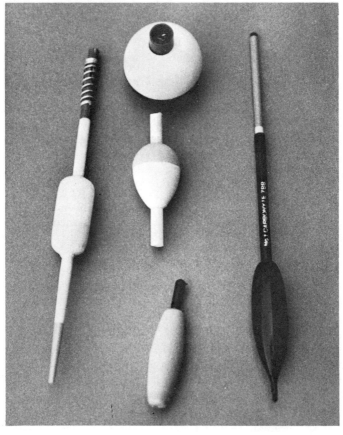

All bobbers are not created equally. Shown here is the pencil-shaped bobber, round bobber, Lindy slip bobber, a foam bobber, and an English Carbonyte float bobber.

The basic idea of the slip bobber rig is that the bobber will slide freely on the line between the bobber stop and the sinker. When casting, the bobber stop will go through the rod eyelets and your reel. The bobber will slide down the sinker. After casting, the bobber will slide back up the line to the bobber stop as the sinker pulls the line through the bobber. This bobber allows you to cast it in very deep water and a greater distance from the boat or shore.

When setting the hook, take into consideration the angle and length of the line. As the bobber goes under, slowly take up the slack in your line until you feel the fish. Set the hook as soon as you feel the fish.

The pencil-shaped bobbers have been around for a long time and they are very popular with a number of the panfishermen. The pencil-shaped design offers less resistance in the water and is not as readily detected by the bluegill as would be the oval and round floats.

This float has a spring fastener that you compress and place the line into a slot. The tension of the spring against the line will hold the bobber in place. The float is easy to use and can be readily seen with its fluorescent finish. I have used them on a number of bluegill trips with success. The spring and wooden slot has caused line abrasions on several occasions, however. You can overcome this abrasion problem by removing the installed spring and replacing it with a one inch piece of surgical tubing and installing a small section of rubber band in the wooden slot. This procedure has not only protected the monofilament line surface from line abrasion but its friction doesn't allow the bobber to slip.

The best American float on the market is the Thill fishing float. These were designed by World Champion float fishing expert Mick Thill. Lindy-Little Joe makes a variety of these floats. My favorites are the Mini-Stealth, Mini-Shy Bites, and the Shy Bites. As the bluegill move into the shallow bays for the spawn, I use my Bionix fly rod or B & M crappie pole, a Zebco Bullet .257 reel, and TriMax 8 pound clear monofilament. The bait is hooked on a size 8 Gamakatsu Aberdeen Bronze hook with a mini Shy Bite (Model SB1). The Gamakatsu hook, Thill float, and soft English shot, which balances the rig, can be purchased from Cabela's and other sporting goods stores.

Controlling the depth is the key with bluegill, unless they are on the beds. I can move the Thill float up and down and find the bluegill. They are ten times more sensitive than round bobbers. This writer personally guarantees you at least double your catch with the Thill float system.

These sensitive floats can be fished tight line or as a slip float. Interestingly enough, there is another method of fishing these floats. It is called lift fishing. On some days the wind never seems to let up. Your float keeps blowing away from your favorite brush pile or boat dock. However, with this method the bait remains near the bottom and the entire float is below the water. When the bluegill picks the worm or cricket up off the bottom, the float surfaces and you know it is time to set the hook.

It is easy to rig for this type of fishing. I thread the float on the line and add the hook. When fishing four to five foot of water, the float is attached four feet above the hook with a small split shot or stop knot. Then enough split shot is added three feet above the hook, but below the float. The final step is to add a larger split shot two inches above the hook. This will sink the float well below the water level. When the baited hook is picked up off the bottom, the float rises to the top of the water and you set the hook.

Another good technique for choppy water is to let the bobber dance on top of the water with your jig or live bait moving up and down below the water level. This bobber is very easy to cast with spinning or spincasting equipment.

A clear casting bubble is a favorite of mine when I am throwing tiny spoons, flies, nymphs, floating and sinking bugs. This small bobber keeps the lure at a set depth so that the bait can be critically worked over the top of weedbeds.

Why Not Use The Best Fishing Knot?

Weak knot and dull hooks account for more lost fish than all other tackle failure combined. Interestingly enough, these two factors are not caused by a manufacturer, but are the result of human error.

Approximately 90 percent of the anglers in this country use the Improved Clinch Knot. This knot has been around for years, and has been passed down from father to son, uncle to nephew, or friend to friend for generations; each angler feeling that they had passed on a very important tradition to the next generation.

After working extensively in the area of monofilament lines and fishing knots for six years on some very expensive professional testing equipment, I have come to realize there are better knots available for the public.

When I first began testing knots, I made the same mistake many line manufacturers continue to make today; testing my knots with dry line, rather than using wet line. When I started comparing my dry knots with knots tied in line soaked in lake water, the results were astounding. Wet monofilament slips more in the finished knot than does dry line.

Of the most frequently used and easy to tie fishing knots available to the public today, I was eager to find out which knot was the most reliable. I designed an experiment to find out an answer to that nagging question.

Five of the most popular brand of monofilament in the United States were selected and purchased randomly from sporting goods dealers from the east coast, Florida, Alabama, and the midwest. All of these spools of line were cut into 2 1/2 foot lengths and then soaked in lake water for 24 hours.

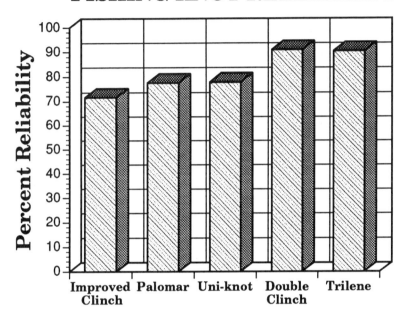

FISHING KNOT RELIABILITY

Some fishing knots are better than others. The Improved Clinch knot is one of the worst, however with one additional step this knot can become one of the best. It is called the Trilene Knot.

The five knots chosen for the study were the Improved Clinch, the Uni-knot, Palomar, Trilene and Double Clinch knot. While the test used only these five knots, dozens of other knots have been tested in the past, and none of them compared to these five, or were simple enough to tie so that they would be accepted by the fishing public.

Each of the five knots were tied 25 times into each of the brand lines, then broken one by one in an Instron Tester, which measures the pound force to break the knot. A total of 625 knots were tested.

After each knot was broken, a new understanding of knot behavior started to unfold. The myth of a 95 to 100 percent reliable knot only existed in the minds of those that wanted to believe such an idea.

Before I confuse all of you, an explanation of the term "reliability of a fishing knot" is needed. The reliability of a knot is calculated by dividing the fishing knot's break strength by the same break of fishing line without a knot. Interestingly enough, after a few knots were broken, I learned very quickly that a fishing knot produces one of the weakest links in your tackle system.

The least reliable knot that I tested was the Improved Clinch knot, which had an average reliability of only 71.7 percent. From past experience, I knew that this knot would slip when pressure was applied by a fish. The lab results showed this to be true because it tallied 55 slips, 65 knot breaks, and only five line breaks.

The Palomar knot had an average reliability of 77.6 percent. It is a fast knot and very east to tie. The Palomar knot never slipped in 125 tests! However, the knot broke 104 times, and the line broke only 21 times. Line breaks are what you are striving for in a knot, because the line should be stronger than the knot.

The Uni-knot was the third knot to be tested. This knot has been touted as the best all around fishing knot system. However, the results gave it only a 77.9 percent reliability. The wet Uni-knot had 35 slips, 79 knot breaks, and only 11 line breaks.

The Double Clinch knot was able to top the 90 percent reliability barrier. This knot had an average reliability of 91 percent. Five slips, 44 knot breaks, and 76 line breaks were recorded. The knot is awkward since a doubling of the fishing line is necessary to make this knot. If using lures with small eyelets, this knot often times cannot be used.

TRILENE®KNOT

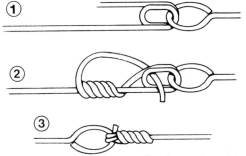

Drawing courtesy of Berkley and Company

The knot that showed the most promise was the Trilene knot; testing a 90.4 percent reliability. The knot had only five slips, 62 knot breaks, and 58 line breaks.

The Trilene knot basically is the same as the Improved Clinch knot, except one additional step is made that makes this knot much stronger. Instead of going through the eye of the hook once, the tag end is brought through a second time. The six line wraps then are completed and the tag end threaded back between the eye and the two coils that were produced.

High quality knots tied in wet premium nylon lines stack the odds in the fisherman's favor and minimizes the risk of break-offs and line failures.

CHAPTER 6

Live Bait and Chemical Fish Attractors

As Joe Hughes from Rebel Lures walked down a boat dock toward his bass rig, he spotted four children, ages ranging from 4-7 years, with a string and a small hook. Joe asked them if they were fishing and the kids agreed that they were but their father wouldn't give them any bait. Upon further questioning, Joe learned that the father wouldn't buy any bait because he would have to clean what they caught.

"Do you want to catch some bream?" asked Joe with his Arkansas draw. All of the kids (two boys and two girls) agreed they wanted to but their wasn't any bait.

Well, from that point on Hughes gave these young anglers a lesson in finding live bait they won't forget for a long time.

"Around this dock their is a thousand baits available just waiting to be picked up," smiled Hughes. He walked over to a light post and thumped a moth with his finger and promptly put it on the little girl's hook.

The moth sunk very slowly in the water and a big bream came out from under the dock and sucked in the moth much to the surprise of the squealing little girl.

Joe left the eager little anglers and went to the grocery store. Upon returning, he met their father who was blocking the dock. "I want you to see what you have done," said the father who was actively engaged in the cleaning of bluegill. The grumbling father had about 25 bluegill staring him in the face.

Hughes looked around and every light post was picked clean of moths. The kids were hooking bluegill faster than the father could clean them.

Joe is trying to make the point that their is plenty of free bait, just for the taking. However, as Joe will be quick to point out, catching bait is one thing and keeping it alive is another.

Keeping and Finding Bluegill Bait

"If it weren't for bad luck, we would have no luck at all!" is a popular HEW HAW saying, but it is a poor excuse for a fisherman. Many anglers believe that fishing is luck. Fishing today is a game. A game of knowing fish behavior, fish movements, their structure requirements, and their food habits. Anglers must know all the rules of using such tools as rods, reels, hooks, lures, lines, and live bait effectively.

Each year anglers pour out millions of dollars into the U.S. economy by purchasing all types of live bait. The minute that these anglers walk out the store is generally when their troubles or "bad luck" starts. Frisky minnows, squirming worms, jumpy crickets, and slithering leeches catch fish and lots of them, I might add. So what can you do to make "good luck"?

For an answer to this question, I directed my questions to Ray Goodman, owner of Timberline Fisheries in Marion. He is a wholesale live bait dealer for all of southern Illinois, and if Goodman doesn't know how to take care of thousands of dollars in live bait, then he goes broke.

"Worms," said Ray, "are the easiest to keep alive and the easiest to mistreat and destroy." I always thought that you could treat all worms alike but not so according to Goodman. The large nightcrawler, which is used for bass, bluegill, and catfish, is called a "cold worm". A "cold worm" can be stored in the refrigerator down to 34 degrees fahrenheit. Driftworms (a nightcrawler's smaller cousin) and mealworms (a beetle larvae) are also called "cold worms". The popular red wiggle is not a "cold worm" and should not be stored below 45 degrees.

"Worms purchased in the spring have few problems," said Ray. "Fishermen who keep them out of the direct sunlight have very active worms. However, when air temperatures soar on past 80 degrees several steps should be taken to keep these worms alive. A thick insulated cooler like a small minnow bucket is best. If the air temperature hits 90 degrees and doesn't seem to stop, some crushed ice in a sealed plastic bag should be laid on top of the worms. This will keep them alive and very active all day."

If you want to keep "cold worms" alive for future fishing trips, sprinkle a little cornmeal on the top of the bedding material and put them in the refrigerator.

Having "conditioned" worms is vital. Most worms are too soft to stay long on a hook if they're taken directly from the earth or out of a store. You can generally overcome this problem by "hardening" the worms for a couple days prior to using them. Place the worms in a box of straw, sawdust and dry earth. They'll lose moisture, toughening the skin, making them more durable on a hook.

A styrofoam container will keep nightcrawlers cool and very active. Crushed ice in a sealed plastic Ziploc bag should be placed on top of your worms when the temperature hits 90 degrees.

Most anglers would rather buy their bait than try and find it. However, avid bluegill chasers like to catch their own.

Worms are strictly nocturnal creatures and will not appear during daylight hours unless their would be a heavy rainfall chasing them from their holes. So for many of us, that means we have to seek them out on their terms which is nightfall.

Vacant grassy lots, parks, and home lawns are excellent places to start your searching pattern. They are always easier to find after or during a rainstorm. Some of the best crawler hunting that I have done was during summer thunderstorms.

I have always found that a headband light with a small battery pack to be ideal. This light keeps both of your hands free to catch the worms. It is not unusual to get into an area that has up to a dozen worms present. Your first grab can yield four or five of these crawlers. I tape a red, plastic cellophane over the lens so they won't spook. Always pick your worms into a container full of worm bedding rather than a empty bucket which will pack the worms causing injury.

You must become a sneaky crawler to get a crawler. These creatures react quickly to vibrations caused by your footsteps. I prefer to use tennis shoes or better yet go bare-footed. When I get into an area filled with worms, I get down on my hands and knees to catch them.

Worms seldom completely exit their holes. Sometimes only less than an inch of the worm is protruding from the hole. Removing them can be easier if you coat your fingers with sawdust. Quickly grasp the worm and pull with slow steady pressure to get the worm out of their burrow. A quick pull will tear the worm in half. Done correctly, you'll pop the worm out before it can re-anchor itself in the ground.

For proper raising techniques of these worms, I suggest you read "Facts About Nightcrawlers" by the master of worm growing, George Sroda. The book can be purchased for $5.00 from Magic Products, Inc. Highways 10 & Q, P. O. Box 33, Amherst Junction, Wisconsin 54407.

A dedicated worm fisherman is an artist. He practices his sport with the delicate skill of a superb seamstress. I have seen anglers thread a wiggling worm on a hook with such skill that the fish would never have guessed that the tasty morsel contained a hook.

There are several ways to rig a hook. Each angling method requires a particular technique. For example, if you are going to troll for bluegill near weedline, the hook would be inserted through the head or under the collar so it streams behind. This rig can be enhanced by adding an ultra-small spinner blade and split shot ahead of the worm.

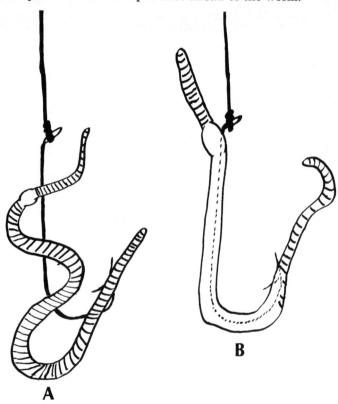

Most anglers hook a worm several times (A). Bait stealing bluegill are caught by burying the hook inside the worm (B).

Most panfish like a bait that is suspended in the water. Loop the worm two or three times over the barb of the hook. I prefer to just barely hide the tip of the hook in the worm. Add your bobber above the squirming worm. Flip your wrist as soon as you see the bobber slip below the surface.

"Crickets keep best at 70 degrees," said Ray who was trying to hold a handful of brown crickets like a hand grenade. Goodman added, "They can be stored in a garage upon returning from a fishing trip provided that the temperature in the garage is above 50 degrees. If the temperature is above 90 degrees, the crickets will have to be given water in a lid. Cotton or a paper towel should be placed in the water filled lid to keep them from drowning. It is best to put them in a darkened air conditioned room."

Crickets can be easily kept for your next fishing trip if you feed them grass, lettuce, sliced potatoes, or chicken mash. If crickets are kept for very long, they should be supplied with water in a shallow dish which has been filled with cotton to keep them from drowning.

Crickets are not that difficult to raise. I use a garbage can which I have waxed or polished the top 12 inches. This will keep the crickets from crawling out. However, I prefer to use a window screen to cover the top.

Crickets are hooked behind the collar and through the back by most anglers.

A six inch layer of fine, clean, damp sand is placed in the bottom of the can with four to six inches of straw on this. I add about 50 crickets to the can. Supply the crickets with chicken mash and water (add the cotton to keep the young crickets from drowning). In the fall or early spring it may be necessary to put a light bulb in the can to keep the crickets alive.

These crickets should lay their eggs in the soil and hopefully in less than 25 days they should hatch out. The young crickets should be large enough to use in less than two months if kept fed and well watered.

Grasshoppers are a very good bait during the summer and early fall. During the day, they are difficult to capture. However, after dark they are easily captured with a headband light. I use an old milk carton punctured with small holes to collect the hoppers. They are easily grabbed by hand and it is not uncommon to capture several hundred in a few hours. Excess hoppers are frozen in plastic Ziploc bags for future fishing trips.

The folks down at Reelfoot Lake love to fish with cockroaches when they can get them. They are found in old barnes and houses, garbage dumps, and other places. You can easily trap them in containers with raw vegetables, apples, or fresh bread. They are very active at night, so run your traps early the next morning.

In college I raised them in my room in gallon jars with cheese cloth over the top of the container. Provide them with hiding material on top of a wood chip base. I fed my pets fresh lettuce for moisture and a mixture of one cup flour, one half cup dried milk, and one package of baker's yeast.

Recently, I have been able to buy odorless Bluebottle fly maggots from Midwest Direct Live Bait, 859 Manor Drive, in Minneapolis, MN 55432. These larvae come in a variety of colors. These will keep up to four or more weeks in a plastic container in a refrigerator at between 32-38 degrees Fahrenheit.

Maggots are free for the taking all during the summer months. Just hang a piece of meat or filleted bluegill carcass outside and the blowflies will be visiting your meat within minutes. The larvae should be big and plump within less than a week. Put them in corn meal and they will clean up their act so to speak and become more pleasant to use. Use a small 10 hook for baiting.

I have known some anglers to find a road killed raccoon and hang this from a tree over the water. As the blowfly larvae fall from the carcass, the bluegill are attracted to this free meal. These anglers slip back within the week and fish near falling maggots. I am not sure of where a good gas mask can be purchased.

Meal worms make very good bait for bream. You can find them where grain is stored such as grain elevators, feed stores, or granaries on a farm. Meal worms are the larvae of grain beetles which lay their eggs in the grain.

Gall worms are found in golden rod stems. When the eggs are laid in the stems by a wasp, the tissue swells and forms a very hard gall. The larvae is found in the center of the gall. The galls will keep for several months in the refrigerator. This bait is readily available in the late summer, fall and winter months.

Small larvae are found within the swollen stems of goldenrods during the fall and winter months.

"Leeches may be ugly to you, but to a hungry catfish or bluegill they are pure heaven," Ray grinned as he slipped his hand into a container of slithering leeches. "In the northern states, leeches are a popular live bait for bluegill. They are very easy to keep alive. Put them into an insulated bucket with very damp bedding material and keep them out of direct sunlight. Upon returning from a fishing trip, dampen the bedding material and store in the refrigerator." That should really make the wife happy, I thought.

Live bait that has been taken care of properly should make you a "luckier" fisherman. Now, all you have to do is to worry about getting wiggling worms on the hook.

Chemical Fish Attractors

I think that we are entering into a new and exciting era of fishing. This new frontier is so new that very few scientific experiments have been done on smell and taste in freshwater gamefishes. A number of investigations have been conducted on sharks, catfishes, salmon and a number of minnow species. The data derived from all of these studies show that smell and taste are of immense importance in the feeding behavior of all fishes in general.

For a bluegill to smell its food, water currents bearing food odor molecules must pass into the bluegill's anterior nostril and into the olfactory organ located below the nostrils. Unused odor molecules pass out the posterior nostril.

Fish have paired nostrils which contain the organs of smell, the olfactory organs. The nostrils have two nasal pits, one pair on either side of the head between the eye and the tip of the snout. These olfactory organs do not open into the throat of the fish but instead into "blind sacs". Water currents continuously enter the anterior opening and pass out the posterior opening of each nostril.

Inside each nasal pit is found a membrane-like tissue that is complexly folded in order to increase the total surface area for smell. According to Dr. Mike Howell, Chairman of the Samford University Biology department, "when activated, these receptor cells discharge small bio-electrical impulses to the olfactory (smell) centers of the brain where the odor is interpreted as "food" or "non-food" odor. If it is a "food" odor, this may cause the fish to exhibit feeding behavior."

Scientific studies have shown that as a fish reaches an older age, these olfactory folds increase in number. For example, a 4 to 6 inch bass usually have from 5 to 7 olfactory folds. However, a 12 inch bass might have 8 to 10 folds, while a 20 inch bass will have nearly 20 folds. Researchers at Samford University believe that the older and larger bass have a better developed sense of smell.

The nerve cells for smell extend from the fish's nasal sac into the front of the brain. The smell will lead the fish to the bait. The receptors for taste, however, can be located in and around the mouth area as well as over its body. These nerve cell extend from the taste bud to the back portion of the brain. Therefore, according to Dr. Howell, "Smell is a

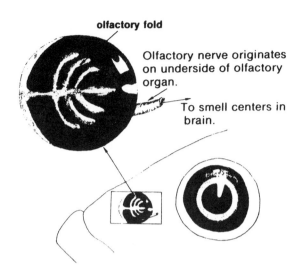

olfactory fold

Olfactory nerve originates on underside of olfactory organ.

To smell centers in brain.

The olfactory fold when activated sends small bio-electrical impulses to the smell centers of the brain.   Drawing courtesy of Keeper Bait Company.

more long-range or distant sense, while taste is the nearby, or contact sense."

Taste experiments have been done on a variety of fish species and many have been found to react to bitter, salty, sweet, and sour tastes. Human saliva and extracts of earthworms have been shown to cause a strong taste response. This points out that spitting on a bait can improve your fishing. However, these experiments showed that fish react very strongly to amino acids. Amino acids are the major components of protein or flesh.

Experiments by Japanese workers with the red sea bream and the conger eel showed that these species were very stimulated by an amino acid called L-glutamine. Brain wave activity was also very high for L-methionine and L-alanine. Many of these amino acids show favorable responses with rainbow trout, carp, brook trout, whitefish, and Atlantic salmon. Even though I have not analyzed these products, one company admitted to me that amino acids are used in their chemical attractor. Interestingly enough, catfish and bullheads with their taste buds on their barbels respond positively to L-serine with L-glutamine.

It is not my intent to confuse you with all this chemistry, but instead to point out that ground work has been laid to market products which might make your fishing trips more productive. A new frontier of fishing may just be in the area of amino acids.

Several companies are developing chemical fish attractors for anglers. At first many of us have been very skeptical as to the effectiveness of these products. However, now I feel that some of these products really work.

Scientific evidence was scarce several years ago when Berkley & Company began research into the mechanisms that trigger fish to strike. Berkley researchers focused on the fish's senses, particularly the senses of smell and taste. Their findings are intriguing.

Fish use smell and taste to find and engulf food, and many trophy fish are taken on live bait because it has a favorable smell and taste. The bait appeals to fish and fools them into feeding.

According to Dr. Keith Jones, Berkley fish researcher, "There are two main considerations when fishermen select a fish scent: 1) how effectively does it disperse into the water, and 2) how effectively does it trigger fish to strike?

Regarding dispersion, a true fish attractant should disperse into the water slowly, giving off a trail for fish to follow.

Many formulas are oil-based and do not mix in the water. These do not attract fish, but merely cause the fish, once it bites, to hold onto a bait longer. They appeal primarily to a fish's sense of taste.

A water soluble formula can actually attract fish. It must, however, be designed to time-release into the water, and this is where many formulas fail. They come off the bait the instant it hits the water and are ineffective. Dr. Jones states, "Berkley Strike's active ingredients disperse slowly into the water. It has time controlled releases."

The chemical composition of a scent determines its effectiveness. According to Dr. Jones, "Berkley research has focused on the triggering mechanisms that cause fish to strike. Berkley Strike is more than just a set of chemicals that smell and taste like food. We sought to sensually stimulate fish to feed, to overpower their inhibitions. Berkley Strike appeals to both the fish's senses: smell and taste.

Recently, Berkley has added a new product called Berkley Alive. This is a major breakthrough in the application of chemoreception in fishing. Stored as a dry powder, when applied to a wet lure, Berkley Alive duplicates natural fish slime. Berkley Alive gives a lure or bait a natural feel and taste and contains a potent long-lasting fish attractant that emits odors in a time-controlled manner. It is easily applied to any wet lure or bait. It's so effective in duplicating a fish slime that care should be taken not to get it on wet hands or equipment.

During some of the experiments with chemical fish attractors, I found that they would reject some of the liquids. I would use sterile round cotton balls that would sink when they were dipped in liquid. On one occasion the round cotton ball was expelled with such force that it looked like Halley's Comet exiting the mouth of the crappie. Before you could say a thousand one, the cotton ball, which had been dipped with a popular chemical attractor, was blown out of its mouth with such force that the cotton ball had a tail like a comet. The fish wanted nothing to do with the cotton ball dipped with this particular chemical attractant.

A 16 ounce bluegill prepares to suck in a cricket that has been sprayed with a chemical fish attractor.

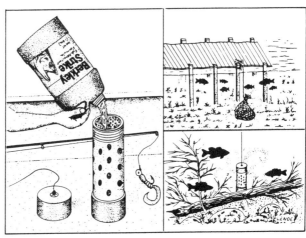

Fish attractants offer potential to increase your catches. Place attractant on your lure, or where legal, attract fish to your dock, boat or a favorite brushpile by mixing attractant with dry dog food or kitty litter in a mesh bag. For the same effect, saturate a sponge placed in a holed pipe.

Experiments have been conducted on bass. Lester Jack Windsor of the Biology Department of Samford University has researched the chemo-reception in bass. His bass experiments were done by lowering the control vial and later the Fish Formula II vial into the center of a metal ring. During this time, the experimenter stood behind the blind unseen by the bass. The vials, one by one, were gently lowered into the fish tank by a 4 pound test monofilament fishing line tied to each vial. Each of the vials would remain in the center of the ring for five minutes.

During this time, the reactions of the bass to the vial were recorded. Each time that the bass would cross the ring to investigate the vial it was recorded. After a period of thirty minutes, the second vial would be lowered into the ring and the number of bass crossing the ring was recorded.

In each test tank they had different numbers and weight sizes of bass. His experiments showed that bass are usually attracted to either food or non-food objects introduced into their territory. That probably comes as no surprise to you or me, because when I am diving the bass will always come to seek out the disturbance in their territory.

Windsor did find that groups of equal-sized bass were strongly attracted to Fish Formula II. However, in groups of unequal-sized bass the fish were all attracted to Formula II, but the subordinate bass are kept away from the source of the odor by the dominant bass who usually established a territory around the vial. The larger and more dominant bass became more territorial and aggressive in the vicinity of Fish Formula II and exhibited food-searching behavior.

Experiments with 12 equal-sized bass showed 51-65% more crossings into the ring area when the Formula II was present. When four unequal-sized bass were present, their was almost 26% more crossings. Their would probably have been more except the dominant bass kept the smaller bass away from the vial. Interestingly enough, when Windsor plugged the nostrils of the four unequal-sized bass, their were only 1.3% crossings. This demonstrated that smell was playing a very important role in their behavior.

Windsor went on to show that the tank-held bass do not "rush" over to an introduced object containing Formula II, but instead they unhurriedly and lazily swim towards it. Even though they are only three to four feet away, it might take a minute before the first bass arrives at the object. Windsor feels then that the bait with the Fish Formula II applied to it should be fished slowly. He thinks that this fish attractant would be more effective on worms, lizards, and jig-n-eel lures. Windsor adds "these baits should be used in structure areas which likely hold bass."

The judge of all this all new chemical fish attractant will be you and me. If we can put more inactive fish on our stringers, then we will continue to buy and use the product. It may be one more important tool in the angler's tackle box that we can't leave home without. My tackle box will always have a bottle when I go fishing for any species.

CHAPTER 7

Reelfoot Lake World's Best Bluegill Lake

As you slip your jon boat onto this placid body of water called Reelfoot Lake, you can't help but have a feeling of great expectations. The calmness and beauty of the lake, as well as the excitement of fishing rushes over your body. However, it hasn't always been as peaceful as your trip will be this morning.

Twenty thousand acres of water were rudely and violently created out of chaos starting on December 16, 1811. But it was on the 7th of February, 1812 that the New Madrid fault violently slipped along its geological fault thus putting the finishing touches on this area.

It was a little before four o'clock in the morning when a Chickasaw Indian dog started barking. The tribe members were huddled under their fur blankets trying to keep warm. The dog will shut up in a few minutes. He must have heard a deer down near the creek. Sunrise would be in only a few short hours, won't it?

Without warning the animal-skin lodge shook to the ground. The earth started moving as it never had before. Wildlife had sensed even before the violent quaking that something was wrong, very wrong indeed. The tremor didn't gently alert the area to its gathering force, but instead it unleased its violence as never before.

The Mississippi river with its huge wall of water (described as being 15 or 20 feet in height) sliced and knifed its way into the newly forming lake basin. Fissures and gaping cracks in the earth vomited forth sand and water in such volumes that only angels in heaven could measure.

Many of the lakes and ponds which once covered this area were now sitting high and dry several feet above their past banks. Rumors among some of the settlers indicated that in the Indian country across the river their might be a huge body of water. It might even be 100 miles long and five or six miles wide. The depth of this body of roiling water could only be speculated.

The rumors were correct. A new lake had been created at the expense wildlife and vegetation. From such a violent act, mother nature created beauty and one of the nations best bluegill lakes.

Anyone knows how to fish for bluegill. You just put a worm or a cricket on a hook and add a small bobber, and the rest is history. Right! Not so according to some of the guides who live on this lake.

Al Hamilton with a hefty stringer of Reelfoot Lake bluegill.

"What ever you thought you knew about bluegill fishing, forget it when you come to Reelfoot," said Al Hamilton. This guide and owner of Arrowhead Lodge on Reelfoot Lake at Hornbeak, Tennessee, wasn't kidding. Hamilton has been guiding on this lake since the age of 12 and that was 25 years ago. He guides customers about 100 days a year and in that time he has put together a wealth of information on bluegill behavior.

My trip to this earthquake born lake was greeted by a cold front that moved the bluegill off the beds. Crickets and live worms would not coax these scrappers into a feeding mood. However, Hamilton issued a spinning rod and reel with a small black bodied Beetle-spin on the business end.

"When a front comes in like this it will move the fish off the grass line and beds, so I like to cast parallel to the grass line letting the lure fall to the bottom before I start my slow retrieve," he said.

On the first two cast he had a nice 10 ounce bluegill and a fresh water drum. Within minutes we both had picked up a number of bluegill that we could not tempt with live bait. Several different species of sunfish and a three pound bass fell for my Beetle-spin in the next two hours.

"Fishing is best from March through June," advised Hamilton. "However, seventy percent of the bedding bluegill are caught during mid-May. Excellent fishing continues through June. During March, however, crickets just won't work on these fish. Artificial jigs and red worms are the best. As the insects start hatching during April through June, cricket fishing is great."

Many of these bluegill will average about ten ounces. However, you will take several that will be near the pound mark. You will soon learn that Reelfoot Lake bluegill grow very quickly in the rich delta waters. You will note on the graph that a five year old fish has stopped growing in length and started putting on weight. A five year old Reelfoot bluegill tips the scales at close to nine ounces and fish that size are hard to find on most lakes. The only lake that will give up close to that average is Horseshoe Lake in southern Illinois.

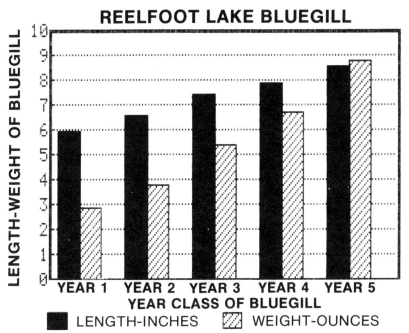

REELFOOT LAKE BLUEGILL

LENGTH-WEIGHT OF BLUEGILL

YEAR CLASS OF BLUEGILL

■ LENGTH-INCHES   ▨ WEIGHT-OUNCES

Al went on to tell me that it may be hot during July and August, however, many good bream are caught along the edges of the grass line, lily pads, and in the shade of the cypress trees. Usually one or two bluegill are taken around these trees during the summer, whereas during the spring you might catch thirty to forty hand-sized fish.

Hamilton loves a good summer thundershower because the bluegill will go on a good feeding spree. A slight rise in the lake water will turn the bluegill on, but falling water signals slow fishing.

True to Al Hamilton's words, this lake was very different to fish. Most bluegill lakes that I have fished you would find the bluegill bedding within inches of the shoreline. However, here we found most of our beds ten to fifteen feet away from the shoreline in three to five feet of water. Al looks for green colored water with a sandy bottom rather than the areas which contain black-stained water.

It may be hot during July and August, but many bluegill are caught in the shade of the Cypress trees.

Hook size is important to Hamilton. He prefers a long shanked #4 hook in a dark blue or black finish. A short shank #4 will work but it is more difficult to unhook a big bluegill if he takes it deep in his throat. If he were in an area with smaller bluegill, then he would use a #6 or #8 hook. Hamilton also likes to add a florescent red bead above his hook to attract bluegill.

Adding a red bead above your hook can be very effective in attracting bluegill to your bait, but not all guides like to use this technique. One of these guides is Bennie Smith.

Guide Bennie Smith nails another bluegill with a Lew Childre "Bream Buster" pole. Anglers can still rent the antique Reelfoot boat that Bennie is sitting in.

The next day I fished with Bennie Smith out of Boardman's Resort at Hornbeak. The 47 year old Smith has been guiding for 37 years on this lake. His entire living comes from this lake. As we boarded the famous Reelfoot Lake boat which is driven by a gasoline engine inside the boat and a propeller protected by a metal shield under the boat, Smith indicated that the fishing was going to be slow with the cool north wind.

We motored into a spawning area and drowned our crickets for over an hour before moving on. Smith wasn't concerned about out lack of action and predicted that as the sun warmed the water we would start filling the cooler. Bennie kept moving from one place to another searching for some hungry fish.

"Most anglers that come to this lake make two mistakes. First they will set on a bed or two all day long hoping the bluegill will come to them. Second, they will catch thirty to forty fish a day and soon realize that if they had hired a guide the first day they were on the lake, their catch rate would easily have been close to 100-150 bluegill. Most of these fish would have ranged in size from 8-16 ounces," Smith pointed out.

"See those frothy bubbles," Smith noted, "drop your cricket in there." No sooner had the cricket slipped below the water surface and the pencil-shaped bobber was gone. A hefty 12 ounce bluegill was cutting circles in the water. Seconds later this fat male bluegill was being iced down. Bennie went on to tell me that he finds many bluegill beds by locating these frothy bubbles. According to Smith, when the males start cleaning these bedding areas of algae and debris, he takes this material into his mouth and spits it out as a foamy mass which rises to the surface. He knows that he has narrowed the search for his bluegill down to this area.

Bluegill are found along the edge's of the canal. Look for the fish along the weedlines and any fallen trees.

Smith had taken me onto a point that had some hollowed out cypress stumps. Each of these stumps gave up at least four to six mean bulls starting to prepare the spawning bed. "That stump will be good for catfish," smiled Smith. His sentence was just being completed as a two pound catfish pounced on my live cricket. My Lew Childre Bream Buster glass pole was bent double as I challenged the catfish in his territory — a mean root infested stump. Unfortunately, the catfish did not come out the winner. You will string up more than one catfish during your stay. I hope your fishing line is strong enough to hold them.

Bennie prefers to use live crickets over worms and on inactive bluegill he will use the fish attractor called Fish Formula II. Smith noted that recently he was using this fish attractor on a very slow day. His client did not care to spray the liquid on his cricket until Smith had put over forty bulegill in the boat and the visiting angler had five fish. As soon as the client started spraying the Fish Formula II, the action started for him. Hamilton points out that the anise smelling fish attractor is just another tool to have in your boat to catch more fish.

Reelfoot Lake is the world's largest earthquake made lake in the world. Over one million visitors come to this lake each year to fish for crappie, bass, bluegill, yellow bass, and catfish. It is probably one of the few areas of the country that I have traveled that the entire family will go home with fish.

The area has 16 privately owned dock and motels. Many of these resorts also have camping and RV facilities. Visitors will also find a state park with lodging accommodations. The state of Tennessee also has 10 areas on the lake for camping.

Families can find a number of things to do in this area besides fishing. Horseback riding, go-cart riding, scenic water cruises, bird

Most spawning beds are found in deeper water away from the shoreline.

watching, movies, museum, antiques, amusement park, historic sites, ferry, nite clubs, tennis courts, golf and much more. You will also find boats to rent, people to clean your fish, fish fries, good places to eat, and other attractions. The lake contains 56 different species of fish and the shoreline area is inhabited by 240 different species of birds. Bald Eagle tours are given daily from November 1 through March 15.

Why not give the 20,000 acre lake a try? The unexcelled beauty of giant cypress trees, the lore of Indian burial grounds, many family activities, and the very exciting jumbo bluegill fishing will make a very interesting family vacation.

The entire family can join in on the bluegill fishing at Reelfoot Lake. The author's daughter, Karin, holds up a stringer of 12-14 ounce bluegill.

CHAPTER 8

Taking The Mess Out of Cleaning Bluegill

"How do you want to clean your fish, southern style or yankee," asked Al Hamilton of Arrowhead Lodge on Reelfoot Lake. I never really thought much about cleaning bluegill in those terms, yet these two methods are very different.

I'm sure not very many of us can say that we relish the idea of cleaning our catch after a long hot day on the lake. However, someone has to do the deed or you proudly take the fish next door to your neighbor and give him your prize catch. Chances are he will like the good eating but not you for bringing the stringer over to him at eleven o'clock that evening.

Fish properly taken care of are superb eating. The preservation of the flavor of fish starts the minute that you put them into the boat. Most livewells were not designed to hold 50-100 bluegills. One of the worst villains contributing to bad fish flavor is the common metal stringer. An angler strings freshly-caught fish and forgets about them, assuming that they will be alive when he returns to the dock. What usually happens is that the fish die from a combination of too much sunlight, too little oxygen, and extreme stress. When this occurs to your catch, the flesh of the bluegill becomes soft and the flavor suffers.

From experience, fishing experts recommend either keeping freshly-caught fish alive and out of stress situations, or immediately cleaning the bluegill and placing them on ice. Live holding methods include the round, wire basket which many panfish anglers use. However, the wire basket must be sunk in water deep enough to keep the fish cool and shaded from sunlight. Don't put too many bluegill in the basket or overcrowding will cause stress and result in bruising and general deterioration.

I highly recommend that when these fish are caught, they be placed immediately into a cooler of crushed ice. This will keep the fish chilled. Firm flesh is also easier to clean when you arrive home. If you do return home at a late hour, you could pour another bag of ice over the fish and clean them the next morning. The fish will lose some flavor but the quality of these fish are still quite good.

How To Clean Bluegill Southern Style

This method of cleaning fish is the older of the two methods. This method is quite good but it has one major disadvantage, and that is the final product is left with all the bones which can present a big problem with small children. However, it is the easier of the two methods to learn for the beginning angler.

The following steps should get you through a mess of bluegill in record time.

Start at the tail end of the fish and begin flipping the scales from the sides of the fish.

Step 1. You can buy a commercial fish scaler with teeth or a large tablespoon will work quite well. Start at the tail end of the fish and begin flipping the scales from the sides of the fish. A number of newspapers placed under the bluegill will catch most of the flying scales and this will make clean-up much easier.

Step 2. Remove the head by angling the cut from behind the head and gills to the belly area. A good sharp knife is needed here to cut through the backbone.

Step 3. Slit the belly and remove the intestines. For many anglers this is as far as they will go in dressing their catch and these fish will fry up quite nicely. However, I like to remove the dorsal and anal fin. This extra step will remove many small bones from the flesh. If you freeze your catch in Ziploc bags like I do, the removal of the dorsal and anal fin will prevent these bones from puncturing the bag and leaking water into your freezer.

Remove the head by angling the cut from behind the head and gills to the belly area. Slit the belly and remove the intestines.

How To Fillet Bluegill Yankee Style

The most preferred method of cleaning bluegill is the filleting method. This method not only produces boneless fillets for the entire family to enjoy, but the end product will take up less room in your freezer. You will also find that these fillets freeze very nicely in Ziploc bags which lay flat and stack in your freezing unit.

Step 1. Make an incision from the top of the fish, around the gills, and stop at the belly. This cut will be one quarter to one half inch deep on bluegill. Insert your fillet knife where you made your beginning cut. The point of the knife should be touching every rib bone as the knife is brought back towards the tail of the fish. You will feel the knife tip touching each rib.

Step 2. Pull the flap of meat and scales back near the head of the fish. Gently remove the meat from the rib cage with the tip of the fillet knife. Some anglers cut through the rib cage

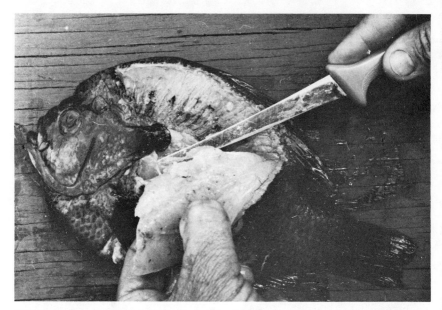

After making an incision from the top of the fish, around the gills, and stopping at the belly, the point of the knife touches every rib bone as the knife is brought back towards the tail.

bones but all that does is dull your knife blade very quickly. You will find that the meat slices very easily away from the rib cage.

Step 3. The knife is laid at the back of the rib cage and with a sawing-slicing movement, the knife blade follows along the top backbone until the knife reaches the end of the tail. Leave the fillet, skin, and scales attached at the end of the tail. If you detach the fillet, it makes removing the flesh more difficult.

Step 4. With a sawing-slicing movement, work the knife from the tail to the head of the fillet. Your knife should glide over the top of the skin without breaking it. A flexible knife allows you to do this with little difficulty. This is probably the hardest part of filleting a fish and you will cut through a few skins and scales before you learn to glide the knife under the flesh. Stick with it, the worst is over.

Flip the fish over and repeat the above steps. You will soon be able to fillet bluegill in less than a minute with a little practice. Don't give up just because you "butcher" a few of your first fish. Even very small bluegill fillets will yield some very tasty potato chip-sized morsels.

Electric knives can clean a mess of bluegill in a jiffy. Some anglers that are terrible with fillet knives are a craftsman with an electric knife.

With a sawing - slicing movement, work the knife from the tail to the head of the fillet.

Fillet Knives - Your Key To Successful Fish Cleaning

Most beginning filleters choose an incorrect sized fillet knife. Blue-gill need a four inch flexible knife blade. I highly recommend three knives that are more than adequate for getting the job done.

Buck Knives makes an excellent four and one half inch knife that is called the StreamMate. This knife is made of high-carbon steel to hold an edge. A big selling point of this knife is their specially engineered handle shaped to fit your hand. Their knife is made of textured Kraton which has a tacky finish to eliminate the danger of slipping, no matter how wet the handle becomes.

Chicago Cutlery has a superb flexible four inch knife featuring a curved handle made of solid American Walnut with a blade which pivots on a single solid brass rivet. This folding fillet knife has a lock-back feature that prevents the blade from snapping shut if bumped while in use. It has an excellent flex for parting the flesh from those tricky rib bones. The knife blade is made of a special blend of high carbon stain-less steel which resists rust, staining and pitting. In all my years of cleaning fish, I have never seen a fillet knife that was so sharp as this one. Since the knife folds, it fits compactly for storage in any tackle box.

Electric knives are super for filleting bluegill and one knife has been truly designed with the angler in mind and that is the Mr. Twister Electric Fisherman. This electric knife features an extra powerful motor which oscilates the blades faster and lasts much longer than conventional knives. It has a comfortable grip and convenient trigger which makes this knife easy to handle. The blades are made of stainless steel which zip through the bones and meat very quickly.

A Sharp Knife Is The Key To Cleaning Success

Either of these two methods of cleaning your catch will sooner or later give you a very dull knife. If you don't cut any bones, generally one good sharpening will last you through fifty or sixty bluegill. However, if you use the southern style of cleaning, be prepared to sharpen your knife several times.

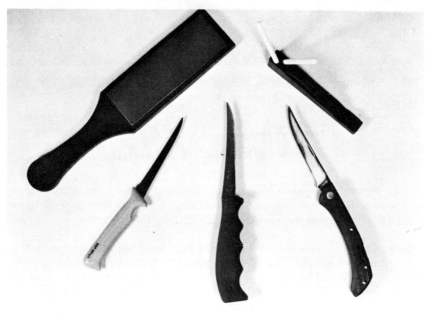

A flexible fillet knife and a sharpening stone or stick is needed to clean a mess of bluegill. The Lindy-Little Joe knife, Buck's StreamMate and Chicago Cutlery's folding fillet knife are very good buys. These can be sharpened on an EZE-LAP diamond stone or a Chicago Cutlery Crock Stick.

Anglers today have a variety of sharpening devices available to them. Almost any sporting good store carries natural stones, carborundum blocks, ceramic sticks, and industrial diamond stones. All of these will sharpen knives, however, I have found through experience some are better than others.

Their are two sharpeners that will get the job done with very good results. One of the best sharpeners to arrive on the scene in the last few years has been the industrial diamond knife sharpeners. The EZE-LAP Company, 15164 Weststate, Westminster, California, makes this space age sharpener which has an array of unique diamond crystals which yield a fast-cutting surface. Their surface is a precision steel substrate covered fully and evenly with diamonds. These diamond crystals will not pull out and the surface will not dish or groove as in the carborundum stone. A fine diamond surface is recommended for maximum sharpening. I have found that any angler can put a very sharp cutting edge on a knife in about one half the time of the other sharpeners.

The angle that you lay your knife on a stone will determine the sharpness of the blade and how long an edge will remain. A ten degree angle for filleting fish is perfect. This edge will last a long time provided that the angler does not cut through the rib cage bones. This angle edge is so sharp that it will shave the hairs on your arm. If you cut through the rib cage bones, then you will need a twenty degree angle on your blade.

Anglers should grip the knife securely and apply pressure as you draw the blade across and down the stone, as though you were cutting a piece of meat. Then reverse the knife and make the same stroke in the opposite direction, carefully maintaining the angle of attack on the other edge bevel.

My recommendation is that you experiment with the angle that best suits your needs. However, keep the sharpening angle identical on both sides of your knife.

The Crock Stick sharpeners have been out for several years. They are designed for the angler who has trouble consistenty laying the knife at the exact angle every time he makes a lap. Chicago Cutlery has brought out over eight different styles for the sportsman that allows for trouble free sharpening of your favorite fillet knife.

To sharpen a knife blade, the two Crock Sticks (white alumina ceramic rods) are removed from the holder and placed in the slanted holes of the base. The unique pre-set angle takes all the guess-work out of sharpening. The knife is sliced downward with a slicing motion. The knife blade is alternated from one ceramic rod to the other. The blade is held straight up and down when you make the slicing motion because the correct rod angle has been determined for you. You will produce a sharp and even edge on your blade.

Freezing The Catch

The length of time that you can store fish in the freezer depends upon its protein and fat content. High protein fish like bluegill will keep longer in the freezing unit than will a high fat fish such as trout and salmon.

A fish wrapped in freezer paper or aluminum foil will keep for a couple months, however, since you have cleaned up on several good spawn beds, you will probably want to store all of these for several months. You can store your catch in old milk cartons filled with water.

Freeze the bluegill fillets in a Ziploc freezer bag filled with water.

However, over the years I have had excellent success with storing my bluegill in gallon size Ziploc plastic bags. I put enough bluegill into each bag that I know my family will eat at any given meal. I cover the fillets with water all the way to the top of the container leaving just enough head room for ice expansion.

When freezing the fillets, I use about a 2 1/2 percent brine solution. This is made by dissolving 1/3 cup of table salt in one gallon of water. These fillets will keep up to a year via this method of storage. When you are ready to defrost the fish, let the package thaw slowly for 24 hours in the bottom of your refrigerator. If you are in a hurry, thaw the fish in a sink full of cool tap water.

Some anglers will wrap their fillets in heavy aluminum foil. The foil will provide a very good vapor and moisture resistant barrier to freezer-burn. Place these foil wrapped fish in a plastic bag. Suck all of the air out of the bag before you tie it shut. You will want to keep the frozen air from touching the fish fillets because oxygen causes the fish flesh to discolor and become rancid.

CHAPTER 9

Be A Master Bluegill Chef

Fish, high in protein, moderate in calories and carbohydrates, is a nutritious food that is often misused in preparation. Many of the families that "don't like fish" have probably never eaten properly prepared fish. Most angling families are blessed with a bountiful supply of bluegill and other panfish. They can and do have fish any day of the year thanks to our improved storage and freezing facilities.

Small lean fish such as bluegill can easily lose some of its flavor through over-cooking and high heat. The true secret of cooking fish is the quick searing at the start of the baking, broiling, or frying which helps to retain the flavorful moisture of the bluegill.

This chapter is divided up into several sections of bluegill preparation. My family truly enjoys properly prepared fish. When they sit down to a meal, I get the comment "Oh, no we are guinea pigs again tonight!" Generally the new recipes are quite good. The recipes in this chapter have been screened by some very picky eaters.

Fried Bluegill

Most people tend to underfry or overfry bluegill. When this happens, you get your choice of grease soaked fish or a tough, chewy piece that lacks any flavor and is probably burned on the outside.

Fish chefs fail at frying fish because they do not regulate the frying temperature. An electric skillet, Coleman camp stove, electric or gas stove, and the new propane fish cookers are excellent at regulating your grease or oil temperature. A cooking thermometer is a must for frying fish.

Properly prepared bluegill should be fried at the correct temperature. Tasty fish which have a cornmeal, a cornmeal and flour, or dry bread crumb base should be fried at a temperature of 360 degrees. My uncle, Ray Lemme of Lincoln, Illinois, discovered many years ago this critical fish frying temperature. Ray found that this temperature seals the cornmeal and flour thus preventing the grease from soaking into the fish's flesh. Undercooked fish will be grease soaked and overcooked fish are generally dark brown on the outside and lack moisture on the inside. Recipes that involve pancake flour. Bisquick, cracker crumbs, and flour should be fried at 340-350 degrees.

Nothing beats a platter of golden fried bluegill.

Skillet Bluegill

2 cups	Flour
1 cup	Cornstarch
1/2 tsp.	Salt
1 can	Premium Beer

Add enough of the premium beer to the above ingredients to make a mix similar to pancake batter. Buttermilk can be substituted for the beer. Fry at 350 degrees until golden brown.

Sweet and Sour Bluegill

8-10 Bluegill Fillets	
1	Egg
2 tbs.	Premium Beer or Water
1 cup	Dry Bread Crumbs
1 envelope	Oriental Chicken Seasoning Mix
1 jar	Commercially Prepared Sweet and Sour Sauce

Cut the bluegill fillets into strips or nugget-size pieces. Dip these pieces into the egg and beer mixture and then pat with the seasoned bread crumbs. Fry at 360 degrees until they are a deep golden brown. The cooking process will take about 2-3 minutes. If you cannot find any oriental chicken seasoning mix, use an Italian flavored bread crumb mixture. These excellent strips or nuggets can be served with the sweet and sour sauce as an appetizer or as the main meal.

Italian Fried Bluegill

10-14 Bluegill Fillets	
1	Egg
1 tbs.	Milk or Buttermilk
1 cup	Flour
1/2 cup	Dry Bread Crumbs
1/2 tsp.	Oregano
1/2 tsp.	Salt
1 cup	Crisco Oil

Remove chilled bluegill fillets from the refrigerator and pat dry with a paper towel. Beat egg and milk together. Dip the fish into the egg mixture and then roll in your mixture of flour, dry bread crumbs, salt and oregano. Fry in the Crisco Oil over medium-high heat (350 degrees) until golden brown on both sides.

Buttermilk Bluegill

10-12 Bluegill Fillets	
3 cups	Buttermilk
1 box	Aunt Jemima Buttermilk Pancake Mix

Few people drink buttermilk, but in this recipe it cannot be tasted. The buttery-flavored milk enhances the flavor of the bluegill. Place the bluegill fillets in a bowl and cover completely with buttermilk. Let stand for one hour, add the pancake mix to a brown paper bag and remove the fillets one at a time from the bowl. Shake off excess milk, and shake them lightly, four fillets at a time, in the bag until well coated. Lay fillets in a skillet containing 1/2 inch of cooking oil that is not quite as hot as is used for deep frying (the milk solids will clarify and burn) and fry until golden brown all over, and crispy around the edges. Drain on absorbent toweling.

Fellow outdoor writer, Kay Rickey of Buckley, Michigan, donated this recipe from her excellent book, "SAVOR THE WILD". The book is filled with fish, big and small game, and gamebird recipes from some of the most well known outdoor writers in the United States. You can purchase this excellent book for $13.00 from Sportsman's Outdoor Enterprises, P.O. Box 192, Grawn, Michigan 49637. The following recipe was given to her by my friend, John Weiss.

Bluegill Tempura

10-12 Bluegill Fillets

1	Egg Yolk
2 cups	Ice Water
1/2 tsp.	Baking Soda
1/4 tsp.	Salt
1-2/3 cups	Flour
4 cups	Crisco Oil
1 small jar	Sweet and Sour Sauce

Combine egg yolk, water, baking soda, and salt into a medium-size mixing bowl. Beat until the mixture is frothy. Gradually add the flour, mixing until it is well blended. Use the batter as soon as it is mixed.

Pour the oil into an electric skillet to a depth of 2-3 inches. Heat the oil to 375 degrees. Cook only several fillets at one time. You might even want to cut larger bluegill fillets into strips for easier frying. Remove from the grease when the fish are a golden brown and drain on a paper towel. Serve the bluegill while they are crisp and crunchy with a sweet and sour sauce.

Baked and Broiled Bluegill

I am not fond of baked fish. However, one can tire of fried fish and that is how new recipes come about. Through trial and error and suggestions from a few of my friends, a few good baked bluegill recipes begin to surface.

Bluegill Italiano

10-12 Bluegill Fillets

1/4 tsp.	Oregano Leaves (dried)
1/2 tsp.	Basil Leaves (dried)
1/4 tsp.	Black Pepper
1 cup	Mozzarella Cheese (shredded)
1 jar (16 oz.)	Rague or Prego Spaghetti Sauce

Arrange the fillets in a large baking dish after pre-warming the oven to 350 degrees. Pour the spaghetti sauce over the bluegill fillets. Sprinkle the fillets with oregano, pepper, and basil. Spread the shredded Mozzarella cheese over the fillets. Bake for about 20-25 minutes or until the fish flakes very easily. You will enjoy this one!

Bluegill Parmesan

Mrs. Mary Lou Goodman of Carbondale, Illinois came up with this delicious recipe which she uses to fry trout. It may be good on trout, but it is even better on bluegill.

10-12	Bluegill Fillets
1 cup	Dry Bread Crumbs
3/4 cup	Parmesan Cheese (grated)
1/4 cup	Chopped Parsley
1 tsp.	Paprika
1/2 tsp.	Whole Oregano
2 tsp.	Salt
1/2 cup	Melted Butter or Margarine
1/2 tsp.	Pepper
Lemon Wedges	

Clean, wash, and dry fish fillets. Combine bread crumbs, Parmesan cheese, parsley, paprika, oregano, basil, salt, and pepper. Dip bluegill in melted butter and roll in bread crumb mixture. Arrange bluegills in a well greased 13 x 9 inch baking dish. Bake at 375 degrees for about 25 minutes or until the bluegill flakes easily when tested with a fork. Serve with lemon wedges.

A shore lunch of freshly caught bluegill is possible when you're camped in a location like this. Photo courtesy of Coleman Company

Broiled Shawnee Bluegill

A lot of the broiled fish that I have eaten were rather tasteless. The following recipe makes a plate of bluegill taste very good.

2 pounds	Bluegill Fillets
2 cups	Buttermilk
1	Egg (beaten)
1 tbs.	Milk
1 tsp.	Paprika
1/4 cup	Parmesan Cheese
2 tbs.	Flour
1/4 cup	Butterbuds or Melted Butter

Soak bluegill fillets in buttermilk for 12-24 hours. I always keep dried buttermilk on hand, but fresh buttermilk gives the fillets a better flavor.

Wash the fillets with water and discard the buttermilk.

In a shallow baking dish line the bottom with aluminum foil (shiny side up) and spray with Pam.

Dip the fillets into a mixture of one beaten egg and one tablespoon of milk.

Arrange the fish in a single layer and sprinkle with black pepper.

Dust the fillets with one teaspoon Paprika, 1/4 cup Parmesan cheese, and two tablespoons flour.

Pour 1/4 cup Butterbuds or melted butter over the fillets.

Bake at 350 degrees for 20 minutes.

Barbecued Bluegill

My good friend and superb outdoor writer Al Spiers of Michigan City, Indiana passed on his favorite recipe to us to enjoy. It is a winner!

Spier's Barbecued Bluegill

10-12	Bluegill Fillets
3	Spanish Onions (very large)
1 tsp.	Garlic Salt
1/2 tsp.	Salt
1 tsp.	Pepper
1 stick	Margarine or Butter
1 bottle (18 oz.)	Open Pit Barbecue Sauce

Heavy cooking foil (18" x 12"

1. Spread butter heavily in the middle of the sheet of foil. A 4″ x 8″ area is needed.

2. Lay whole onion slices (3/8 inch thick) over this buttered area.

3. Arrange fillets on top of the onion slices.

4. Sprinkle garlic salt, salt, and pepper heavily over the fillets.

5. Slice another layer of onions and lay on top of the fillets.

6. Place another layer of fillets on top of the onions.

7. Season heavily again.

8. Pour the Open Pit barbecue sauce over the fillets. Let the sauce drip down the sides of the fillets.

9. Fold the foil over the onions and fillets. Pinch the foil seams together.

10. With a toothpick, poke two small holes in opposite ends of the foil.

11. You can either put the foil pouch on a barbecue grill, open fire, oven, or gas grill.

12. When the steam starts exiting the vent holes, your fish should be done in 10-12 minutes.

13. Unfold the foil pouch, dip the fish in its own juices and sauce and enjoy.

Smoke Cooking

Ideally, food should be as much fun to cook as it is good to eat. However, barbecuing can be in the "no fun" category because it requires tending the fire, turning the meat or fish, and a constant basting to prevent burning and drying.

You can now enjoy the great outdoor flavor in your food without handcuffing yourself to your grill by using the Brinkmann Sportsman Smoker (which also doubles as a barbecue grill).

Aside from the delicious flavor of smoked food, the Brinkmann Smoker takes care of all the work. You don't have to tend the fire, turn the food, or even baste it. This smoker is also excellent with hams, turkeys, ducks, geese, ribs, roasts, and many other meats.

Smoked Bluegill

6-8 Whole Bluegill	Pepper
Salt	4 Slices of Bacon

Rinse the bluegill fillets and sprinkle the cavity with salt and pepper. Brush the fillets with oil or melted butter. Arrange on the cooking grill over the water pan filled with 3 1/2 quarts of hot water. Top each fish with a strip or two of bacon. Cover and smoke the fillets for 2 to 3 hours or until the fish flakes with a fork. You might want to brush the fillets with Open Pit barbecue sauce.

Smoked bluegill are not only easy to cook, but with the Brinkmann smoker they taste so good.

Photo by Kris Wunderle

Appetizer

Appetizer's will get your party off to a good start. Tom Rollins, Executive Director of the Southeastern Outdoor Press Association, passed on a very good recipe by Allen Lee for Bream Cocktail.

Bream Cocktail

2 pounds	Bream Fillets
1 quart	Water
1/4 cup	Salt
1 jar	Cocktail Sauce
Lettuce Leaves	
Lemon Wedges	

Bring enough salted water to cover the bream fillets to a boil. When water is boiling, drop in bream and bring back to a boil. When water is boiling a second time, time for exactly two minutes. Drain off water and cover fish with crushed ice. Line sherbet glasses or small bowls with lettuce leaves. Divide the bream among the dishes and top with cocktail sauce. Serve with lemon wedges.

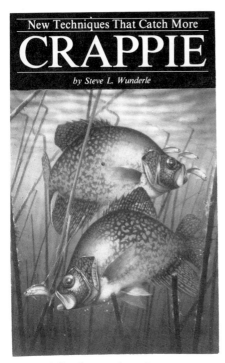

"Advanced Crappie Secrets"

Never before seen photos of crappie feeding underwater and how they stimulate other crappie to feed. New research on catching crappie during a cold front. A new study reveals best way to hook a minnow for more action which will entice a crappie to strike. Catch suspended crappie schools during the hot summer months. Minnow scales falling through the water will stimulate a crappie school to become a feeding machine. New research on fishing jigs will put the luck into fishing. *First Edition on Sale For $6.95* **NEW!**

"New Techniques That Catch More Crappie"

Never before has a fishing book been written and fully illustrated with on the lake graph recordings of crappie movements during the spring, fall, and winter. Between the pages of this book anglers will find a new system of crappie fishing which uses the latest in crappie research and fishing tips from professional anglers and guides! Special chapters on how to catch pre-spawn crappie, tough summer fishing, and where to find them in the fall and winter. Over 30,000 copies sold! *On Sale For $6.95.*

"New Techniques That Catch More Bluegill"

This is the first Bluegill book ever published! You will see and learn how bluegill feed underwater, where and how deep they spawn, where they go in the summer, and many important fishing tips and techniques. Special chapters on how to find and catch spawning bluegill, tough summer fishing made easy, fishing live bait and its care, bobber research, chemical fish attractors, cleaning your catch, and many more tips written for the bank fisherman and the small boat owner. Over 20,000 copies sold, 6th edition! *On Sale For The Low Price of Only $6.95.*

— —

Steve Wunderle Outdoor Books
86 Eight Mile Prairie Road   Carterville, Illinois 62918

_____**"Advanced Crappie Secrets"** at $6.95 plus $1.50 for postage and handling ($8.45).

_____**"New Techniques That Catch More Crappie"** at $6.95 plus $1.50 for postage and handling ($8.45).

_____**"New Techniques That Catch More Bluegill"** at $6.95 plus $1.50 for postage and handling ($8.45).

_____**"Crappie Cookbook-From Lake To Table"** at $6.95 plus $1.50 for postage and handling ($8.45).

_____**Save!** Buy any **two** books for $13.00 plus $1.50 for postage and handling ($14.50).

_____**Save!** Buy all **three** books for $19.00 plus $1.50 for postage and handling ($20.50)

_____**Save!** Buy all four books for $25.00 (Postage and handling pre-paid)

Name _____

Address_____

City_____ State _____ Zip_____